Praise for *The Doing Good Model: Activate Your Goodness in Business*

"*The Doing Good Model* is built on a solid truth: that our definition of success must include well-being, not only for individuals but for the workplace. Based on thirteen specific values, Shari Arison expands our understanding of what it means to do well in business, and shows that if leaders build their companies around these values, there will be a powerful alignment between their own well-being, the companies' bottom line, and the good of the planet."

Arianna Huffington
Chair, President, and Editor-in-Chief,
Huffington Post Media Group

"Shari Arison's book shows how enlightened business leaders who align positive economic, social, and cultural business values into their core business practices have the potential to transform our world."

Dr. Rakesh Khurana
Marvin Bower Professor of Leadership Development,
Harvard Business School

"Shari Arison's example of practicing moral responsibility in business is one that we want to share with our students, as they begin the next phase of their lives. Our vision for our graduates is that they will be engaged and ethically-oriented citizens, committed to building a just, free and prosperous world. Shari's work shows how this can be done."

Dr. Ángel Cabrera
President, George Mason University

"*The Doing Good Model* is a necessary call to action, and provides a powerful lesson to next generation management about how philanthropy and business go hand in hand. Shari Arsion's vision for an ethical corporate world is as inspiring as it is achievable."

Dr. Gregory Unruh
Endowed Professor Doing Good Values,
George Mason University

"*The Doing Good Model*'s practical approach enables people from any background to effectively voice their values and positively act on them, drawing the best from them, fueling creativity, confidence, and skill."

Dr. Mary Gentile
PhD, Author of *Giving Voice to Values: How to Speak Your Mind*
When You Know What's Right

"Touching on the many dimensions of negotiation strategy and planning, the *Doing Good Model* brings enormous impact by making values-based connections that bridge different outlooks. As it ripples out across the world, the model promotes the ultimate goal of win-win situations in business."

Dr. Karen Walch
Emeritus Faculty, Thunderbird School of Global
Management of ASU

"Within just a few days of the Doing Good Model workshop, I saw a definitive shift in people's use of words, and in their openness and sharing of values. I saw true transformation."

Debra Wheat
Executive Editor, Values + Sustainability,
Nomadic Learning and Lead Ambassador
for the Oath Project

THE
Doing
Good
Model

ACTIVATE YOUR GOODNESS
IN BUSINESS

Shari Arison

BenBella Books, Inc.
Dallas, TX

Copyright © 2015 by Shari Arison

BenBella Books, Inc.
10300 N. Central Expressway, Suite 530
Dallas, TX 75231
www.benbellabooks.com
Send feedback to feedback@benbellabooks.com

Printed in the United States of America
10 9 8 7 6 5 4 3 2 1

Library of Congress Cataloging-in-Publication Data:
Arison, Shari, 1957–
The doing good model : activate your goodness in business / Shari Arison.
     pages cm
  Includes bibliographical references and index.
  ISBN 978-1-941631-23-2 (hardback)—ISBN 978-1-941631-24-9 (electronic)
  1. Social responsibility of business. 2. Business enterprises—Moral and ethical aspects.
3. Business ethics. 4. Corporations—Charitable contributions. I. Title.
  HD60.A753 2015
  658.4'08—dc23
                              2014046617

Editing by Erin Kelley and Harrison Flanders
Copyediting by Stacia Seaman
Proofreading by Amy Zarkos and Clarissa Phillips
Cover design by Sarah Dombrowsky
Text design by Publishers' Design and Production Services, Inc.
Text composition by PerfecType, Nashville, TN
Printed by Lake Book Manufacturing

Distributed by Perseus Distribution
(www.perseusdistribution.com)

To place orders through Perseus Distribution:
Tel: (800) 343-4499
Fax: (800) 351-5073
E-mail: orderentry@perseusbooks.com

This book is dedicated to all the chairmen, CEOs, board members, management teams, and employees of the Arison Group business companies and philanthropic organization, as well as the universities and professors, advisors and facilitators, and anyone else, in the past, present, or future, who's been involved in the creation and implementation of the Doing Good Model. You are all greatly appreciated.

Contents

SECTION FOUR
Activate Your Goodness: A Broader Scope of Influence

SECTION FIVE
Platforms for Creating a Better World

CLOSING SECTION

Activate Your Goodness Through Vision & Values

CHAPTER ONE

My Professional Journey

From Caterpillar to Butterfly

Transformation is a subject I have breathed and lived for most of my life. Some people might say I had it easy—I inherited a fortune. But it's like they always say: it's not what you have that matters, but what you do with it. This book is about what I did with it.

I always wanted to make a difference in the world, and I'm on a constant path of personal growth and transformation. Having spent thirty years leading in philanthropy and overlapping the last fifteen years running a global business, I learned that together, these two worlds form a huge platform for positive change. Because my company operates in more than forty countries on five continents with thousands of people in our global workforce, we have an incredible impact.

In order to create long-term sustainable change, I knew I had to engage the right people who formed the right teams to create strategy and implementation. My goal was to introduce a values-based perspective in order to transform all of my business entities, because I knew in my heart even then that all of my holdings would have to be congruent with my own moral compass. I knew this change would be possible with vision, never giving up, and by being a personal example to others.

Anyone who knows me knows that when I have a vision, followed by a deep calling in my gut, nothing will stop my persistence in making it happen. It has taken time, but together we've been able to create a model that has turned into our organizational compass.

Now we have a practical, and yet elated, guide to follow. It's a business model that has grown from within and matured over time, a model that guides us at the Arison Group in our daily work, making decisions and acting upon them. Because we feel that everything we do focuses on doing good, it was easy to come up with a name: *The Doing Good Model.*

The Transformative Power of Doing Good

Doing good gradually became my go-to mantra, and I have found very creative ways to use my platforms to advance this concept of *doing good*. I even initiated an annual event to encourage people to do good, which has grown by leaps and bounds. Last year in 2013, hundreds of thousands of people in more than fifty countries went out to do a good deed for the benefit of others on International Good Deeds Day.

But this book is not about Good Deeds Day. It is about a business model that is values-based and works! I was told very bluntly, years ago, that no large company of mine could be sustainable and profitable at the same time. I was told that I could not develop a culture of corporate giving in a country where no such thing even existed in people's minds.

I was even told, more than once, that I did not belong in business. People suggested to me that maybe I would be better off just running the family's foundation. But you know what? Almost thirty years later, I am even more convinced of my own original vision. I have a lot to offer to the world, and I have had the privilege of leading the most amazing team of forward-thinking executives and employees within my companies and organizations. As a collective, we have taken these companies to new levels of success and prosperity that none of us could have foreseen when we started out.

I don't say this to be boastful—I say it because I want to share how we did it, and how you too can use this same set of values to transform yourself and your own company or organization.

I am passionate about this values-driven business model because I believe that it works well in companies of any size, in any country, and in for-profit or non-profit entities. I firmly believe that anybody and everybody can benefit from adopting a values-based approach to their daily life and work life, whether they are a company owner, a board member, or a worker in any job or field. And I trust that you will believe this too, once you learn more about the *Doing Good Model*.

Creating a Culture of Giving

Over the years as a young adult, I worked in every single department of the company that my father established: Carnival Cruise Lines. Later, I served on its board of directors. This laid the foundation for my business experience. At my father's request, I started and ran the family foundation in Miami, so it was only natural that when I moved to Israel, I continued my philanthropic work by establishing an office there.

From the beginning, I knew I needed to do things differently than in the United States. I set up the Arison Foundation, which was later called The Ted Arison Family Foundation. I introduced professional business practices into our philanthropic organization, something that was not mainstream at the time. We focused on donations that would make a major impact on society. These donations, which we now call social investments, were substantial commitments in the fields of health, education, research, and more.

I was able to be totally involved in every detail from the ground up in these large philanthropic projects. Some of the flagship projects included building a brain research center, the primary medical care facility in Tel Aviv, an arts school for grades one through nine, the Arison Business School, an historical museum, and many more.

Even though I was growing personally and professionally, I still wondered what my true calling was. I have always felt a creative force within me and have always cared deeply about the future of humanity. While still searching for my true purpose, I was able to express my creativity and caring in all the projects that I worked on. The spaces were created to be a family-like environment that is respectful, beautiful, and state of the art.

I also spearheaded a movement toward corporate giving in Israel because I firmly believe that the business world has a responsibility to give back to the communities in which they operate. This is a value that I was raised with. I was inspired by a model of giving that I had seen in the United States, so I brought these concepts and practices to Israel, and I created an organization called Matan (the Israeli United Way). Today, virtually all businesses in Israel participate in corporate giving, which proves that with vision and perseverance, you can create a new culture—in this instance, a culture of giving.

Personal and Business Transformation

As a parallel to the philanthropy I was doing, I launched and ran my own business. Then in 1999, after inheriting a huge empire, I was thrown into the next stage of my journey. I found myself with a diverse group of companies that I had to somehow lead and manage, along with my own business, which involved restaurants. Arison Investments at that time owned a newspaper, an electronics and communications company, and a satellite TV provider, along with more than 50 high-tech and bio-tech companies. After a process of learning about the companies and understanding that they were not aligned with my vision and I could not add to their value, I eventually sold all of them. I also sold my own restaurant business in order to concentrate on leading the enterprises where I felt I could truly add value.

The two companies that I kept an interest in and continued to invest in were Bank Hapoalim and an infrastructure and real estate company called Shikun & Binui. Each of these companies had cumbersome internal business structures that were archaic and did not make much sense in the fast-moving business environment that I could foresee.

It was clearly time for transformation, but changing such deeply held structures and corporate cultures was not going to be easy. There seemed to be no vision at all within these companies, short-term or long-term, and I made it my mission to introduce vision and purpose. Little did I know how long and challenging the process of transformation would be—but what incredible successes we are seeing in those businesses now!

Arison Investments continued to expand, buying out Salt Industries, which we later renamed Salt of the Earth. I also founded Miya, based on my vision of abundance, knowing that one of the most important challenges of our future is ensuring clean drinking water for all.

As you will see in the coming chapters, our group of companies and organizations has expanded and transformed itself in a remarkable way. And out of this process has emerged a unique and comprehensive values-based business model that is applicable and practical for any businessperson who wants to contribute to the growth of themselves, their organization, and the world.

CHAPTER TWO

The Doing Good Model

Early Lessons from the Banking World

Very unexpectedly, at a time when I took my first steps in the banking world, I was appointed to the board of Bank Hapoalim. I did however come onto the board with extensive hands-on experience gained by working in virtually every department within a large international corporation, so I knew how organizations and corporate structures really work. I had years of experience with both for-profits and non-profits, so I came in with that perspective too.

As it turned out, I didn't need to be so nervous about my own financial management savvy, because once I started attending meetings for the bank, I soon discovered—to my surprise—that there were quite a few board members who also came from different business backgrounds.

However, this did not seem to keep them from commenting, objecting, and agreeing about things that they did not specialize in! I can only imagine how management felt when they had to take direction from people on the board who were not from their industry, compared to the management teams who had been working for the bank for ten, twenty, and some thirty years. I wanted to have a dialog based on shared knowledge and productive understanding.

I felt that I couldn't express myself until I learned the material. I took private lessons with people I trusted, and I went to each of the departments to meet with managers and employees to learn the true nature of the business. I constantly referred to a financial lexicon and materials until I became comfortable with all of the terms, and only after a year did I begin to speak my mind at board meetings.

I spent years bringing to the board my own unique way of thinking, being involved with branding, caring for the customer, vision, and giving to the community. Looking back on those early years in my career, I can see how it has contributed tremendously to my understanding of the process it takes to create real transformation in a large organization. The good thing about gaining experience in the banking field is that it gives you an overall view of the economy.

Today I am no longer on any of the subsidiary boards. Although as owner of the Arison Group, I sit on the boards of our privately held entities both in business and philanthropy: in other words, Arison Investments and The Ted Arison Family Foundation.

A Passion for Our Collective Future

I am a lifelong learner and I learn by experience. It is my nature to always strive for improvement, personally and professionally, and to seek ways to contribute to the world around me. I believe that when a company or organization is driven only by financial results, it cannot fulfill its highest potential. There is a bigger picture, and I believe we need to take personal responsibility for the betterment of our collective future, and so do our companies and organizations.

That's why, for as long as I can remember, I have been creating vision after vision for both my personal life and each and every entity in all of my holdings. I instilled these visions in all of my philanthropic organizations, and on the business side, I chose directors to sit on the different boards who care just as much as I do about vision and values while still making a profit. With the leadership of my team, we were able to inspire the different business units to adopt the visions I created. Of course, this was a much easier process with our private companies than with the public companies, where the understanding and the process took many, many years.

One day, after years of vision work, I woke up and realized that all of these separate visions formed sort of a model. As I saw it, each value is a building block, but together they formed a building. Understanding that each of these entities now had a vision, and each vision translated into a value, that's how we came up with ten of the thirteen values comprising the *Doing Good Model*.

For instance, one of the values is Financial Freedom, which came from the vision for the bank. The value of Sustainability came from the vision instilled in our real estate and infra-structure company, and the value of Inner Peace arose from our philanthropic organization, Essence of Life. Some of these values are easier to understand than others. Some are more practical, and others are more spiritual. Feeling that the model was not complete, I added the final three values: Being, Purity, and Fulfillment.

How do you take such elated values and turn them into a model that's hands-on, understandable, and practical? How do you take these values and turn them into a model that will be beneficial for individuals and a collective, whether that collective is a small or large business, a philanthropic organization, or even a country?

Transformation Through Collaboration

When I took over Arison Investments, I tried to bring out the best in these companies while respecting and working with what was already in place. But after seven years, I realized that if I wanted to be aligned with my own moral compass, I would need to make some hard and bold changes. This would involve bringing in new people, expanding the stake of my holdings, letting go of the past, and proceeding in a way that would ensure that I could instill the visions and values while maintaining stability and continued growth and profitability.

This might sound easy, but it was far from that. In order to inspire the transformation of these old-style companies, it took a long process of getting everyone on board. After years of individual vision processes for each of our companies and organizations, it was time to bring everyone together. I asked for a meeting with all of the chairmen and CEOs to discuss bringing all the visions and values together in order to create one model for the entire group.

You must understand that bringing everyone together meant a gathering of representatives from the bank, the real estate and infrastructure company, the salt company, the water company, the family foundation, the volunteer foundation, and the spiritual foundation. Wow, what a group.

Now we had a group of people with such diverse career paths and different goals sitting together, with extremely different points of view, and me wanting them to agree on the meaning of these values, right down to the very last word. The first meeting was a disaster. Everyone was screaming and yelling at one another, no one agreed, there was no understanding—what was the point?

I even got two phone calls after that first meeting telling me that this was not going to work. Maybe I should create this model on my own, just as I did all the visions in the past. I heard this from both the chairman of Arison Investments, Efrat Peled, and the chairman of all of our philanthropic organizations, who happens to be my son, Jason Arison. I explained to both of them that this was a new world of collaboration, and I strongly believed that no matter how long it takes, we would all come to a place that everyone was at peace with our collective vision.

But my son said, "Mom, if you continue with this, you're going to have to give in on your true voice, or the others will have to give in." But I stood fast in my belief that if we put our minds to it, everyone would come out with their own true voice, and together we would find a way to create something that we all agreed on.

Finding the Way

This process took a whole year. During that year, we had many challenges—just scheduling a series of meetings with all of the CEOs and chairmen proved to be quite difficult. We also had changes in leadership, as some people left their positions and new ones came in. We had various facilitators at different times during this process. Some participants got the message and others completely didn't. And yet, at the end of the year, we were all aligned with thirteen written values that we defined together down to the last word. I *knew* we could reach a win-win, and we did.

I realize today that the values in the model are a kick start for values-based conversation and implementation. Although I am introducing these thirteen values, every value that causes someone to grow and do good is, in my eyes, blessed.

After the year-long process, we understood that it was important for each entity to take responsibility for implementation. It's one thing to define values, but it's quite another to implement values in a practical way that reaches every employee worldwide. We set out for another series of meetings.

Meeting after meeting, we tried to determine practical ways for implementation but the frustration just grew higher, and we hit a dead end. At that point, Efrat came to me and said, "Let me and Jason find the way." The solutions they found were quite amazing, both in-house, across the group, and within the academic arena. That's what we'll tackle in the next chapter: the challenge of implementation and how we overcame it.

CHAPTER THREE

The Forums

Finding a Starting Point

I can tell you that it was quite incredible to finally have a definition for each of the thirteen values, words that we all agreed on. It had taken a full year to get to that point, and now it was time to start the process of taking those values and getting each of the companies and organizations to commit to implementation.

Our top corporate leaders tried to work it out, but it was not long before we realized that we were at a dead end. We seemed to be having meeting after meeting, and things were not moving forward at all. It was pretty clear that these meetings were a waste of everyone's valuable time, because the chairmen and CEOs just could not seem to find a way to turn the definitions of these values into a practical implementation plan.

That's when Efrat and Jason came up with a brilliant solution, one we still use today, which is a series of forums that each focus on certain values in order to move them forward. They decided to start with the four values that everyone could most easily agree with and understand: Giving, Volunteering, Sustainability, and Financial Freedom. These were the four values that were already becoming entrenched within Arison Group businesses and organizations.

For example, some of our companies were already strong corporate supporters of the communities we operated in. Many employees were already volunteering. Sustainability was a value that was already living and breathing within Shikun & Binui, our infrastructure and real estate company, which takes on large-scale building projects around the world. Financial Freedom had become the vision at Bank Hapoalim.

As the chairman of our philanthropic organizations, it felt like a natural fit for Jason to lead the forum that focused on Giving and Volunteering. Likewise, since Efrat was chairman and CEO of Arison Investments, she was the perfect person to lead the forum that dealt with Financial Freedom and Sustainability.

Employees for Change

The forums were announced and employees from within each entity were asked to step forward if they felt they wanted to be involved. Because this concept of the forums was brand new, no one really knew what would happen, but a few passionate employees stepped forward and took on the challenge.

The two initial forums started with about seven employees each. There was one representative from each of the main businesses and organizations within the Arison Group. This was the first time that all the businesses and philanthropic organizations came together. In each of the two forums, the small groups sat together, and many people got to know one another for the first time. They talked about what the values meant to them and how they thought they could implement the values in practical terms across the board within the Arison Group.

I did not take part in the forums; however, I was and continue to be updated regularly. I was very adamant that although I agreed on starting with four of the values, it was important to me that the entire model of thirteen values be implemented and that we must find the way. It was understood that it was imperative to make each value practical, understandable, simple, and tangible.

From my past experience, I knew very well that "theory" doesn't transform anything. You have to translate vision and values into practical terms. The only way to create real change is to engage people and get them moving so that they can truly integrate new ideas.

Because the representatives in the forums already had the backing of the various chairmen and CEOs, it then became the role of each of those employees to go back to their respective companies or organizations and implement what was agreed upon within the forums. Implementation was accomplished by planning various activities and projects that supported the essence of the value, which would cause the value to come alive within the business or organization. For example, it was agreed that all employees across the board would go through Sustainability training and Financial Freedom workshops. It was also agreed that all companies and organizations would join in on Good Deeds Day. And of course, many more ideas are constantly being implemented.

It was so incredible when all this began to happen. Within the forums, employees were able to express their voice, make a difference, be creative, and become a part of the bigger picture. The forums also brought the separate companies together as a whole with a common purpose. They each moved from being separate entities to becoming a collective "we," something I had desired for a very long time.

As each member within the forums shared their ideas, challenges, and successes, everyone else was able to learn and share as well. Within a few meetings, the group members were coming up with creative solutions, and before long, they were celebrating and sharing the successes they were experiencing. We even had a couple of Doing Good Conferences so everyone could share what was happening. Even I was amazed!

With so much going on, it wasn't long before more and more people started hearing about the forums, and the numbers of attendees kept increasing. The forums are still operating, meeting quarterly, but when the number of employees grew to more than sixty or seventy people in each forum, it was decided to split the forums, going from two to four forums, in order to keep them effective. We have also begun introducing new forums that are now advancing other values within the broader *Doing Good Model*.

Meeting of the Minds—Business and Academia

Since our goal is to have all thirteen values living and breathing within all areas of the companies and organizations, and we didn't find a practical way to implement them all at once, we needed help. That was when we decided to turn to the academic world. My team at the Arison Group found the right mix of academic partners who could help us translate our model into an integrated workshop that would introduce all of the values.

We found a passionate and professional group of doctors and professors from top American universities including Harvard, Thunderbird, George Mason, and Babson College. They began researching and putting together curriculum through constant collaboration with my team at the Arison Group.

The academic team then visited our operations in Israel in order to see for themselves what was being done, and we were amazed by everyone's enthusiasm and comments. The academic team had never seen anything like this before. They did know of many other companies around the world that were sustainable, for instance, or worked with some of the values. However, they had not seen such a diverse operation of companies in such different fields, including philanthropic organizations, implementing such a wide range of values.

I must say that the academic team is amazing. Through their process of research and their skills as educators, they developed an incredible pilot workshop that was held first for our forum members. The employees from the forums gave their comments as to what worked and what did not work, and what they felt could be implemented in their respective companies and organizations.

The academic team took the feedback from those participants and reworked the workshop, redefined it, and presented it again, this time to the chairmen and CEOs. I took part in that workshop and was deeply touched to see that for the first time, even the skeptics were convinced. The next step was to take the new workshop and engage the next level, including the different boards of directors and management teams.

The *Doing Good Model* workshop, as we call it, gives participants a unique experience of how values impact them individually and within their business and philanthropic lives. I've seen people come out changed. The professors use academic-style business case studies, interactive activities, short videos, and team break-out sessions to keep everyone's attention and really help participants integrate and understand the transformative value that the values have. As a logical next step, we have launched together with our academic partners a train-the-trainers course in order to bring the workshop experience to more and more levels of our organizations.

The Doing Good Endowed Professorship

I invested in an Endowed Professorship at George Mason University in Virginia, USA. in order to advance research into values-based leadership. The research being done has taken on a wide focus. It began by looking into the history of corporate values and how these manifest within the individual businessperson, the organization, and society in general. The research mandate also includes determining the best ways for values to be taught so that the right questions or case studies can be posed to get business students thinking.

The Endowed Professor is also developing practical in-class exercises so that students can understand how various values apply to real-world work situations. This approach to teaching values is a sharp contrast to what was taught years ago, when values and ethics were almost exclusively taught from a theoretical viewpoint within business schools.

It has been amazing to see how well this line of research and exploration fits within the Global Citizenship Course and other advanced leadership training courses that have been developed and are being delivered at George Mason. In these courses, students are being encouraged to rank their own values and clarify the meaning within themselves. In this way, values training in universities becomes a means to an end, and graduates can use their own moral compass as a practical decision-making tool on an everyday basis.

The research and material that is being developed is so important for businesses in today's society, businesses who care about people and the planet, alongside profit. I believe that the way to accomplish this is by values-based leadership and businesses that implement values.

A Broad and Universal Set of Values

I have been told that the *Doing Good Model* takes a much more comprehensive approach to corporate values because it was developed within several different fields of businesses and also a range of non-profit organizations. With the help of the academic team, we can now envision ways that the *Doing Good Model* could be implemented just about anywhere.

Implementing it so broadly gives us inspiration that someday we could contribute to solving even bigger complex social and environmental challenges in our world today.

To truly tackle those issues, it is imperative that all levels of business and society cooperate for the good of all. Each part of society brings different things to the table. The business sector, for example, brings innovation, capacity, and ideas, and business has the resources for implementation. Non-profits bring specialized knowledge, credibility, and networks of people who will work passionately for change. I believe that if we find a way for individuals, governments, businesses, and non-profits to work together, we could create a good future for us all.

Expanding the Circles

As a result of the *Doing Good Model* workshops, our managers and employees are really beginning to connect to the bigger picture. They worked with the first four values through activities that came out of the forums, but now the excitement is spreading quickly, and more and more employees are wanting to engage with the remaining nine values within the model, particularly the ones that speak to their own individual hearts.

It's to the point now that every day, I am hearing stories about employees at all levels of the organizations who are taking on additional values and bringing them alive. The forum for Vitality sprang up at the Arison Group headquarters because health and wellness is such an important issue for just about everyone today. The value of Language & Communication was initiated by our Salt of the Earth company because the management team there wanted to focus efforts to improve internal communications among its culturally diverse workforce.

There has been tremendous interest from people outside of our companies, including some people who have worked for us in the past and who have moved on while continuing to implement the values in their new workplaces. This high level of outside interest has brought us to the conclusion that our All One forum, soon to start, will be made up of both internal employees and members of the public.

The *Doing Good* values have settled into most minds and hearts within our workforce. It's amazing how many conversations about the values are popping up together with creative ideas on how to implement them. For example, I recently attended a meeting of our infrastructure company where they were presenting their yearly review and their strategic plans for the coming years.

The entire management team spoke through a value. Manager after manager stood up and focused his strategy in relation to Abundance, Sustainability, Inner Peace, and so forth. I was surprised and deeply moved! It was fascinating to see how they were taking the initiative to integrate the values into all of their business activities and goals.

Furthermore, the chairman told me that they successfully drilled down their strategic plans to all levels of the company while still using the framework of the values. This approach further connected the management team to the model and was well received by all.

Even outside the company, when we speak to external groups, sharing our approach, they too seem interested in learning more about our values-based model. In fact, I recently spoke to a group of high school teachers at one of their professional development sessions. These were teachers of psychology and economics, and they were inspired and wanted more information on how they could implement the *Doing Good Model* in the educational system.

Although this vision started within my soul, it has taken many people who have been engaged, worked hard, become living examples, and grown the circles of positive change. I am deeply grateful to all the directors, managers, employees and universities, and people who have come on board in order to create real transformation within our businesses, organizations, and society at large.

Although we have done quite a bit already, growth and expansion never stops. Within our many plans for the future, we are developing an online training program in order to share the *Doing Good Model*, making it universally accessible.

So now that you have some ideas of how to implement the model, let me share in more detail each of the individual values, starting with *Financial Freedom.*

Activate Your Goodness Through Individual Prosperity

CHAPTER FOUR

Financial Freedom

FINANCIAL FREEDOM

The freedom (and the desire) to choose, based on responsibility and understanding of the framework of abilities and economic possibilities at any given moment.

The Knowledge and Tools to Make the Right Choices

When the value Financial Freedom came to me, it came from deep within myself. Personally, it was not an expression that I had ever heard before that point, but since developing and sharing the *Doing Good Model*, I have come to realize that "financial freedom" has become quite a common phrase in North America.

This vision came to me because I am always looking for ways to create positive change in everything that I do. In this case, for years I had been contemplating my controlling stake in Bank Hapoalim. What could I do to bring added value in the world of finance? Although I had managed to instill quite a few positive values in the bank when I was on its board, I felt that much more was needed in order to make a real difference in the actions of the bank and the way those actions are perceived by the public.

It has always bothered me that I was part of something that people in general seemed to hate so much. I realize some people had good reasons for distrusting or hating banks, like losing their homes, cars, or businesses, for example.

I felt empathy for people who were up to their ears with loans that they had trouble paying back. Personally, I wanted no part of this, but here I was owning a bank. I kept racking my brain to figure out how I could turn this around. Then it came to me—we could do it by creating financial freedom.

It was the perfect answer to my burning question: what good could a financial institution do for people, its employees, and its clients? The answer was to educate them on how to create financial freedom for themselves!

That's what we set out to do: find a way to give everyone we could the awareness, the education, and the tools to make wiser choices. Our goal was to help individuals better understand their finances, their paychecks, and their actual expenses, and show them ways they could balance it all more efficiently to create their own growth and prosperity.

Financial Freedom Is for Everyone

Financial freedom is a value that is not just applicable to individuals. The concepts work just the same for families, companies, and non-profit organizations. For any person or group with financial concerns, we as a financial institution developed tools to help everyone become responsible and make the changes that need to be made. We understand that the responsibility lies on the financial institution, its employees, and the client; everyone has a part in creating positive solutions for complex problems.

Our approach to financial freedom offers a concrete way to deal with finances that has been proven to work at virtually all levels of life, whether it is personal or for business and organizations. It works because when you are mindful, responsible, and educated about what you have, then you can do the best you can with the resources you do have, be they modest or plentiful. Once you know and understand your financial situation, you can make the right decisions and choices that will open you up to a prosperous life, while living within the framework of what you have.

We have all seen the results of individuals, companies, and even countries that have not acted in responsible financial ways. The outcome and effects of their actions spin out and affect a much broader scope than just themselves. Unfortunately, these effects have created negative impacts. But your life and your business don't have to go down that road, and this value was developed to illustrate a better path. The good news is that with proper information, education, and tools, you can reach your own financial freedom.

Changing the Mindset

So once I had this realization many years ago, I believed this vision could be a win-win. I would be able to stay true to my own personal values, while the bank could help people at the same time. But the general feeling about banks was still deeply negative. I knew people in general tend to blame their bank when bad financial things happen to them; I guess that can be easier sometimes than looking at how their own decisions might have contributed to their losses.

I also knew from experience that people don't tend to look at banks the same way they look at other retail products or services they might purchase. It always boggled my mind that the mark-up on clothing or shoes might be 100% to 300% or more, and yet people still buy those items without a moment's thought about the actual cost to produce and deliver the item. Yet when it comes to paying a bank for the services it provides, people very often don't want to pay anything at all.

Clearly, we had several rather big challenges to overcome if we wanted to shift people's thinking about this, both within the bank itself as well as in the minds of our employees and customers. I wanted everyone to benefit from the shift.

But how could such deeply held views be changed? I felt the only way to really change these views was to create real transformation and help people realize that we are all in this together. We needed to approach this as a partnership where both sides are taking responsibility; we needed to create a win-win for both the customers and the bank so we could all prosper.

That's how my idea of introducing the value of Financial Freedom came about. My management team at Arison Investments encouraged the bank with my vision, and the bank acted on this by finding ways to translate the vision into practical education, tools, and actions for their employees and their customers. When individuals have a better understanding of their finances, they can make the best choices and decisions for themselves, their families, or their businesses.

Creating Financial Freedom

I'm proud to say that my team at Arison Investments, especially my chairman and CEO, were totally with me on this vision, and since they are also board members of the bank, they were able to instill the same kind of excitement and understanding of how important this vision really is. One of the biggest challenges at the bank was to translate the term "financial freedom" into a term that was understandable and accessible with tools for action. Implementing this concept within such a very conservative organizational culture was not an easy process, and it required engagement from all levels of the operation.

It has been amazing to see the number of financial tools that the bank has created in order to assist both the employees and clients. Seeing the growth and success, including an online education network with advanced Internet tools, has given people of all ages access to learn how to independently manage their personal and family budgets.

The bank has since extended these online tools and training sessions to include even more financial solutions that people might need for every stage of life, focusing in particular on major milestones. The bank now has tools for schoolchildren who might be getting an allowance for the first time, and for young adults who are just starting out in their careers. As they settle down, buy a home, start a family, and plan for their children's educations and their own retirement, the bank is with them with tools and training to help them along the way.

As a logical next step, the bank also launched a new personal financial planning service that serves as a major step forward in the quest for financial independence. And even more recently, there has been incredible adoption of financial planning apps that are easy to download and use in everyday situations.

A nostalgic addition to the bank's new branding has been the re-launch of a cartoon character that many adults in Israel knew and loved as children—a character from the 70s and 80s called "Savings Dan." Dan has proved to be a reminder to parents and an engaging and playful character for a new generation of children, to teach them the benefits of saving money for their futures.

Another key focus for the bank has been to support small businesses, whether they are our clients or not, by creating the Small Business Initiative, with hugely successful events and programs, including a national-scale Small Business Day. More than 35,000 small to mid-size businesses participated last year, which raised awareness for their companies, and their overall sales increased by 17% on that day.

At the same time, the bank continues to deepen its community commitment, to the point that the bank, as a leader in the Israeli economy, has become one of the largest donors in the country and a major source of volunteers for non-profit organizations. The branch network gives them a way to reach virtually all parts of the country.

The branches undertake local activities in two main ways. The first is to contribute corporately to worthwhile causes, and the second is to actively encourage and support employees toward volunteerism. In particular, the bank tends to support projects in which it can integrate financial education activities into its giving, helping non-profits and community members to stay financially strong so they can keep up their good work.

From its current leadership position, the bank is able to make a huge contribution in creating financial freedom. It has taken close to a decade of steady progress since I first envisioned "financial freedom," but now I hear endless numbers of stories of the personal impact that is being made, and not just at the bank. We at the Arison Group have implemented this value across the board in all of our businesses and philanthropic organizations.

Financial Freedom in Action:
Getting Ready for Retirement

One of the stories that touched me tremendously is Ilana's story. She has been working in the company for many years now and, in fact, has the most seniority of anyone at our main offices. She supports herself and is nearing retirement. Over the years, Ilana had different roles within our philanthropic organizations, and for the past few years, she has been operations manager for the Arison Group, supporting both the business and philanthropic sides.

I don't usually attend the forums; however, at one particular meeting, I was invited because the forum members wanted to update me across the board on what all of the businesses and philanthropic organizations were doing to implement the first four values, namely Financial Freedom, Sustainability, Giving, and Volunteering.

It was amazing to me to see and hear all that had been done, but I was most moved when Ilana took a spontaneous stand and asked if she could share what financial freedom did for her personally.

"Anyone who knows me knows how much energy I have, how I love to check each product four times, get five price quotes, and sharpen pencils on both ends to save money for the group," she began. "But for me, for my own finances, nothing! I know it might not look that way. I have kept my personal papers neat and tidy in folders for thirty years, insurance papers and all that, but if you asked me what it all means, I could not say. I didn't really know."

By this time, Ilana had our attention. She spoke so candidly and passionately. "Then I came to the financial freedom workshop," she said. "I had begun receiving payments from the national insurance institute because of my age, so I put those funds aside. But with regard to my own insurance and investments, after I attended the workshop, I realized that I actually had no idea what I had and I knew I needed to look into it.

"The next day I set up a meeting with the consultant, the same one who lectured in the financial freedom workshop," Ilana continued. "I brought him in the whole stack of about ten kilos of paper. He went through everything, and I left the meeting with one single plastic sleeve containing ten pages, and I knew exactly what was on each page."

I felt her excitement and enthusiasm as she continued explaining how empowering it was to finally know what she had and how she could better secure her financial future. "I learned to differentiate between an insurance salesman for a particular company and an independent consultant who speaks frankly and lets me know what's best for me," she said. "I learned you can negotiate better commission rates, management costs, and there is a whole variety of programs to consider, especially for my age group, what's more risky and what's less. I feel now that within five years when I want to retire, everything will be in place, because I was able to get this education," said Ilana. "I don't think I would have woken up to it on my own.

"But as it is now, I have made many fundamental changes in the programs and funds that I have, including transferring a substantial amount to a different company that will really help me manage my money well. After all, this is the money that I will have to live on and it is the same for you. I encourage the younger people sitting here to really look at your finances now, while you have time to implement the right changes that will work best for you in the long run," she said. At that point, Ilana turned to me, looking me straight in the eye, and said, "Thank you!"

I was so deeply touched, and I could see the people in the room were too, while listening intently. I was happy that the message and the tools related to financial freedom had such an impact. I was amazed to see that the vision I had and its ongoing implementation had deeply impacted a human being and made a real difference in her life.

The Impact of Financial Freedom

There are many other stories like Ilana's. Let me tell you about the outcome of the financial freedom workshops held at Salt of the Earth, one of our Arison Investment companies. Employees and their spouses were encouraged to attend and learn financial management skills to help them with their personal lives and goals.

The statements that we received after the workshop were personal and moving. One forklift operator said, "My eyes were opened after the financial freedom workshop, and already from the first meeting, there is apparent change and it is a big change—how to manage my affairs and make more informed financial and calculated choices. Following the seminar, I realized that many things rely solely on me. I decided to commit my family and myself to this purpose. We all joined forces and followed the workshop manual."

A spouse who attended with her husband shared her perspective this way: "Our experiences before with finances included stressful feelings and many arguments. This workshop opened my eyes. We got rid of our bank overdraft. Today we have a savings account and everything is under control."

One of our welders at the salt plant said, "I see now that I was a big spender. I have changed drastically. Why didn't I think of this before?"

When I hear these kinds of stories firsthand, I am moved by the impact, realizing that the value of Financial Freedom has transformed the lives of so many people. These changes have occurred not only in the bank and in our other companies, but the circles have expanded through employees, their spouses, and clients alike. When I hear how people talk about how their lives have been changed, I see how genuinely touched and grateful they are, and I think, *wow!*

This all started out with a vision of a new approach I had for the banking industry almost ten years ago. It took years of perseverance and patience, finding the right people with professionalism and heart in order to implement this. I am grateful for the leadership of so many people within our companies to stay the course and to continue advancing and implementing this incredible vision. It is not easy to make such a fundamental shift within such a large corporation, and it is an ongoing process, but I am thrilled that we are not giving up, and there is more understanding and impact every day.

Now, I'd like to show how Financial Freedom has gone beyond the individual, permeating all parts of our businesses and organizations.

Financial Freedom in Action: From Personal to Organizational

For years, I've been thinking about how to drastically de-leverage the loans of my businesses while continuing to grow. I have been watching as people and corporations around the world have become too highly leveraged, taking on too much debt, and then I have seen what kind of effect it has when those debts cannot be paid back. It causes a domino effect of people losing jobs, suppliers going bankrupt, and other harsh economic consequences.

In 2013, Arison Investments wrapped up about ten months of a negotiation process for financing a mega-transaction worth several hundred million dollars. This complex deal was done with my wishes in mind, as the owner, seeing the bigger picture and making sure I could de-leverage quickly and efficiently while ensuring continued growth.

There was an event held between Arison Investments and the funding partners to mark the occasion of completing this agreement, which was specifically structured by my team the way that I wanted. At that event, speeches were given by our CEO and CFO that specifically referred to the values-based moral compass that we use. It was important to us that our new financial partners truly understood where we were coming from and, in this case, how our value of financial freedom was interpreted and applied within this mutually successful negotiation. We felt that by staying true to our values, we created a win-win partnership.

One of the comments from the CFO was, "When we talk about financial freedom—we are talking, simply put, about aligning between desires and capabilities. From our viewpoint, it is an existential value, and the foundation for any wise financial planning or conduct. I am convinced that each of you here have experienced it in action—whether through this loan, or the way it was structured, the negotiation process, the issues brought to the table and insisted upon, or just as long-term partners measuring our operations for the long run. A process like this is intriguing and profoundly interesting, even more so during such challenging times. We are happy to be the recipients of your trust and the faith that you have in us."

He went on to further explain how the Arison Group team interpreted our Financial Freedom value, which you will remember is defined as "the freedom (and the desire) to choose, based on responsibility and understanding of the framework of abilities and economic possibilities at any given moment."

To us, within this negotiation, these words meant two very important things. One was that we would secure only what we needed for this situation, and not more, even though more money was available and we were offered more at one point. We wanted to be responsible and knew how to keep within our limits.

The second important element to us was to set up a flexible mechanism for repayment and get agreement right from the start that everyone agreed to this flexibility, even though it was a rather new and complex arrangement. We wanted to be able to de-leverage this loan over time in a flexible way, a way that we knew made the most sense for our company, given all the economic realities we were facing, and our own abilities.

Our CFO closed his comments by adding, "So, now you know that the primary motivation, which brought about the achievement we're all here to celebrate today, is actually rooted in the profound feeling of pride that we have for being part of a group that not only thinks financial freedom, but implements it by practicing what it preaches."

One of the representatives of our financial partners stood up and shared with us that they felt they were treated fairly within the negotiation process and within the final agreement that was signed. It proved to us that a win-win is not only possible, but really, it's the only way that we want to do business, because it's the only way we will succeed in the long run.

As we continue with our discussion, we continue to follow the moral compass of the *Doing Good Model*, moving now from *Financial Freedom* to *Purity*.

CHAPTER FIVE

Purity

PURITY

The clarity of thoughts, intentions, and actions.

Let Your Thoughts Be Your Guide

Have you ever stopped to think about your thoughts? More specifically, the nature of your thoughts? In order to understand and discuss this value, I would like to ask you to take a moment to look at what you are thinking about and how pure those thoughts might be.

Many organizations use related values like integrity, transparency, and ethics, and I agree, those are extremely important. Those values are related to Purity, but they are only just parts of it. The way I look at it, Purity is a much higher value, an elated value. This was one of the three values that came to me in completion of the model and has been defined as "the clarity of thoughts, intentions, and actions."

You might be saying to yourself that "purity" is a strange word to be included in corporate values, and if so, you would not be alone. There were people on our team who questioned how we could implement such a value in an organization. I find that even before real implementation, just the ongoing discussions around the value of Purity started to create incredible change both in mindset and measureable actions.

So indeed it is not as mysterious or intangible as it sounds. Really, I think if people put their minds to looking at their thoughts, intentions, and actions, then they can see with their own eyes what is pure and what is not pure.

Purity in Everyday Situations

Businesspeople with a pure intention care about people and the planet and strive to find a balance between that intention and their desire to be profitable.

It's not only about pure thoughts. Think of the many types of behavior that can affect you as a human being as well. For example, you might ask yourself, what am I putting in my body—is this good for me or not? What am I listening to? Is it something that is uplifting like music, or is it gossip that is unkind? I think that the more we focus our intentions on being pure, the more purity we draw to ourselves from our environment. It is our choice to make.

Businesspeople, as well as individuals, need to watch their actions and choices so that purity is kept at a high level. For example, businesspeople can negotiate a business agreement in good faith and with fair intent. I know that's not popular today in our competitive world, however, if we want to see a change, as Gandhi said, we must *be* the change.

How do we do this? Just as it says in the value, we start with pure thoughts and intent, followed by pure actions. If this seems to be a challenge to you, I suggest sitting down by yourself or with your team and coming up with guidelines to describe what you feel is fair to yourself and also fair to your employees and externally fair for your customers and for the environment.

It wasn't that long ago that a handshake was someone's word, something they would never go back on, but now few people would finalize any deal without a written contract that their lawyer has approved of. Determine in advance that you want to be the kind of businessperson whom others will trust and then strive for the purity to live up to your own standards.

Being Pure

One thing to notice about Purity is that there are different depths, and what might be "pure" for one person might be different for someone else. So for example, a really strict, straightforward person might be someone who would always tell the truth and would be very kind and very caring, but he also might smoke cigarettes. In this case, he might have purity of thoughts and intention, but the air he is breathing is not pure for his lungs.

The good news is that you don't have to be 100% pure all the time and on every level. In fact, I believe that would be impossible. But you might begin today just by thinking about and talking about Purity. Once your awareness is raised, sometimes that alone is enough to move you closer to becoming more pure and having more clarity in your thoughts, intentions, and actions.

While in the past, businesses could get away with poor behavior in the name of "competition" and "winning at all costs," I truly believe the tides have changed; the successful businesses today are building their reputations and increasing their profits by striving for purity. People are waking up to the realization that they want something better. Businesses are expected to act more responsibly, more caringly, more humanely, and more transparently; they are expected to care about people, the environment, and society in general.

Don't wait until you have a crisis on your hands. Instead, set your purity standard now for your business, your products, and yourself. Then encourage your employees to follow your lead. Once you set this moral compass, it will guide you in making the best decisions.

I have always had faith that being true to my own values would benefit me and my companies. I strive to be as pure as I can, on all levels, and so far this path as worked for me. I expect the same from my management teams and company leaders, and I know they strive each day to be very clear in their thoughts, intentions, and actions, and the performance of our companies has continued to improve. I encourage you to have faith that purity will pay off in profitability. I firmly believe that it will as long as your intentions and actions are authentic.

Purity in Action: Miya

When I founded Miya, it was based on my vision of abundance, since clean drinking water is imperative for the future of the human race. The value of Purity is also very much aligned with water, as I believe that every human being deserves to have an abundant supply of pure drinking water. Purity is also important, in my eyes, to the development and success of Miya.

While Miya was still a young company and developing its world presence, it was involved in a highly complex bid for a water efficiency contract, and the customer happened to be the government of a country. Miya was competing against some of the largest conglomerates in the world in this field for this project, and it was recognized within the company that this was an important project for Miya. It would put us on the map and bring a big "win" to our newly developed team.

But when the technical team and senior managers analyzed the request for proposal, as it was set out by the tendering process, it was clear to us that the solution that was being asked of us was not a viable one. There was actually a much better approach that we knew would work, but it was completely outside the box and outside the very strict parameters of the bidding process. But if we did not follow their detailed approach, we knew we could be disqualified just for that.

However, our management team at Miya made a bold decision to go with their truth and not just respond to the requirements as they were written. Our team did not even realize it at the time, but they were practicing Purity because they knew the project could be done more efficiently and in a better way, one that would be much more cost-effective for the client and for us.

There was a lot at stake and it was a big risk. Our team was understandably concerned we would not win the bid. However, I encouraged them to proceed with our values; whether we won this bid or not, I believed that with this approach we would win in the long run.

Our bid was innovative and represented a whole new way to approach this kind of issue. The client ultimately decided to go with Miya because we had submitted the best bid, the most truthful, and I believe, the most pure.

The benefits of this purity were wide-ranging. Firstly, winning the bid gave the young company a much needed vote of confidence and a way to prove its place in such a competitive industry. It also showed the company that you can do business and still stick to your values.

Leading in this way, Miya's team found out that when they began the work on the ground, the company workers were received with trust and respect.

The caring approach we implemented added tremendous value both in the lives of people and in profitability. Our approach led by pure thoughts, intent, and actions has made Miya a very clear, aligned, and professional company proving that you can do business while caring for our most precious resource, water, and bringing that resource abundantly to humanity.

Purity in Action: TOMS Shoes

Another inspiring example of Purity that I came to hear about is Blake Mycoskie's story. He is the founder and Chief Shoe Giver within the company called TOMS. Blake is also the driving person behind the idea of "One for One," which has become a global movement for good. He decided that for each pair of shoes his company would make and sell, he would donate one pair to a person in need. His company has since given more than two million pairs of new shoes to children in need since the initiative began in 2006.

Like so many initiatives, TOMS began its business and its good works from a humble beginning. In 2006, Blake was traveling in Argentina and could not help but notice how hard it was for so many children there to grow up without shoes. In his mind, the solution was simple. He would create a for-profit shoe-manufacturing business that was completely sustainable, but also make a company policy to donate an equal number of pairs of shoes at the same time.

It was such a successful model that Blake realized that perhaps other vital needs could be met using his "One for One" model. With that he developed the idea for TOMS Eyewear, in which for every pair of eyewear purchased, TOMS would help give improved sight to a person in need, applying the "One for One" model.

I met Blake briefly in South Africa at a gathering of global business leaders that I was a member of, The B Team. Blake gave a short presentation sharing his story, and I was truly inspired. I understand that he is inspiring people around the world, but especially young people, because he wants to help them make tomorrow better by living their truth and passion every day. I believe it all begins with purity and clarity within oneself, and in one's thoughts, intentions, and actions.

Purity in Action: A Creative Way of Messaging

You never know when you might see Purity in action. I was recently watching an episode of an American TV series called *Brothers & Sisters* (ABC Studios).

I was particularly excited with this episode titled "Mistakes Were Made," in which one of the lead actresses, Calista Flockhart, played Kitty Walker, who was a reporter and the co-anchor of a news program. Kitty wanted to save her brother Justin from being redrafted by the American forces and sent back abroad to fight again, this time in Iraq.

Kitty was given an interview with a senator, and she purposely did not ask him about his recent divorce, which was a well-known scandal. She hoped that if she did him a favor by leaving the subject alone, he would do her a favor in return, and she might find a way to help her brother.

Realizing that she had seriously compromised her moral values and her role as a reporter, she apologized on live TV for what she tried to do, going on to say that the senator kept his integrity, while she did not. She thought she would be fired, but quite the opposite happened; she was offered an exclusive TV show because of the increase in ratings.

Kitty's co-anchor stood beside her, stating that he would leave the show if she were to be fired (he did not know about the new position she had been offered, which would leave him out of a job). Instead of taking the exclusive offer, Kitty encouraged the TV station to give the new show to her co-anchor, who deserved it more, and she stepped down from the station.

What I liked about this episode was that the character of Kitty was pure in her intentions, thoughts, and actions, by telling the truth on the air and leaving the show. I am not speaking about the series itself or any other issue raised on that series; however, I was touched by this specific episode because it showed, in my eyes, the value of Purity. When media corporations want to make a difference, they can be creative while taking a stand on values. They can showcase values in real-life situations, portraying these values in a way that will be enjoyable to the public.

When people watch shows like this, it makes them think. It brings everyday moral dilemmas to the forefront while showing positive, creative solutions. This inspires people to take a deep, hard look within themselves. I believe that entertainment can have a true message and can create real change, and we see that many films and TV productions are doing just that. Another great example is the movie from years back called *Pay It Forward*.

A moral compass, in my opinion, is essential in our daily lives at home with our families and within the businesses and organizations we are a part of. Here at the Arison Group, we understand that being guided by the *Doing Good Model* (our moral compass) is a step-by-step process. And with that, we move now from *Purity* to the next value: *Being*.

CHAPTER SIX

Being

BEING

*Harmonious existence with all of the components
that create the whole.*

"Being" in Stillness

When we talk about this concept of *being* in relation to the individual, there is just the here and now, this very moment. Although being is on many levels, what I am doing right in this moment is my whole world. As I sit here and write these words and create this book, if I allow myself to be only in the here and now, I can truly enjoy what I am doing.

But a lot of the time, I think that we tend to miss *the moment* because we do not allow ourselves to just *be*. As humans, too many of us are conditioned to always be thinking about the past or worrying about the future, so much so that we often completely miss the present moment, the here and now. We miss out on our actual life.

Being more present comes with awareness, will, and practice, focusing on what your thoughts are at this very moment. What are your feelings and what is your intention? If you want to enjoy the moment, you have to let go of what is interfering, whether it is thoughts or feelings, and choose to be in the moment.

There are many ways to reach stillness and be in the present moment, and what works for one might not work for another. So each individual has to find their own way, the way that suits them best. I am not here to suggest the way, although there are many books and practices. I am only here to say that it is possible.

Through mindset and practice, you will find whatever works for you to help you become more centered, what brings you more in touch with your own being, and what allows you to live more fully in the present. Being in the present is truly a present, a gift to yourself.

"Being" in the Workplace

What happens so many times is that people don't know how to live in the here and now. The world is moving so fast and changes are happening so quickly. Businesses that are not flexible enough to deal with the present moment might have quite a challenge. Although all businesses have to create long-term strategies in order to succeed, at the same time, they still have to live and work in the present moment. The key to success is to be constantly hands-on and be ready to be flexible every moment of every day in every situation.

I can share with you a simple example of a day in the life of a businessperson. In my own business group, just recently, several excellent employees from different management teams had been offered positions with other companies and the government. I could understand that having such a good workforce, our people would be sought after; however, in my book, the way other organizations lure people behind one's back, in the blink of an eye, is not part of my ethics and was very disturbing to me. However, I decided to change that mindset, understanding that actually this was extremely complimentary to the kind of people we have in our group, people who are very professional and connected to values.

While it was a blow to have them leave, we chose to look at it in a positive light, knowing that they were taking with them what they had learned from us. They could now take that professionalism and knowledge of instilling values in a practical way in organizations and pass that on in other circles beyond our group. How great is that!

This also gave us the opportunity to grow more people from within by moving them forward to management. We had to move quickly, as it was totally unexpected that these people would leave, because we saw them as part of our future.

This experience brought me back to myself, to the moment, understanding that what I needed to do was to breathe deep, see the reality, and make the best of it. Knowing that there is a reason for everything, I could wish everyone involved all of the best.

I believe that it's important to understand that change is a constant; it is a natural part of life and therefore a natural outcome of business. Accepting this fact helps us to be in the now and grow. Being is not static, it is dynamic. The goal would be to be in the moment, understanding that wholeness and being are in constant transformation. By being flexible and going with the flow, we can then deal with situations in a positive way.

Research into Mindfulness

I had heard about mindfulness from several sources, including universities and businesses both in the United States and Israel. But it wasn't until I had a meeting with a researcher from a top university here in Israel that I became interested to know more about the subject. She came to me to tell me that many of the insights I had been talking about for years through the Essence of Life (a spiritual organization of mine) are being demonstrated by researchers through brain research. Being amazed by her comments, I asked to hear more about her field of research.

Dr. Nava Levit-Binnun is the head of the Sagol Center for Applied Neuroscience in the IDC (Interdisciplinary Center) in Israel and the MUDA Center for Mindfulness, Science, and Society. She explained that this kind of training in meditational practices was derived from Buddhist traditions, and that mindfulness training was made popular in today's culture by the American researcher Jon Kabat-Zinn with his Mindfulness-Based Stress Reduction (MBSR) program.

She said that mindfulness was the most researched form of meditation, and continued to say that some consider mindfulness to be a state of mind, while others tend to see it as a specific set of skills and techniques. Her team draws on worldwide scientific research into mindfulness, including the work of Dr. Kabat-Zinn.

Mindfulness can be defined as an intentional practice in which a person accepts and places a non-judgmental focus of their own attention on their emotions, thoughts, and sensations that are occurring in the present moment.

Since my meeting with Nava, I've been hearing more and more about mindfulness and how it is being implemented around the world in various circles, including business. My excitement stems from the fact that I have a deep spiritual belief that if each individual—starting with myself, of course—will connect to his or her own essence, together as a collective, we will create a better world.

Connecting to Oneself

Meditation, or as I call it, introspection, is a way to connect to oneself. It is an uplifting realization to me that mindfulness has been researched and proven to do that. I feel that it is extremely important that each one of us create awareness within ourselves, and mindfulness helps some to achieve that.

Mindfulness breaks down the barriers by offering people a way for inner connection that speaks to them in practical scientific terms.

With that knowledge, I organized a workshop to be delivered by the team from the university for my top managers, from both Arison Investments and The Ted Arison Family Foundation. There were people who meditated daily, people who had never meditated, some who could sit quietly, and others who were jittery in their seats. Some have a spiritual outlook and others believe only what is proven scientifically. What was amazing to see was that everyone benefited. Even those "non-believers" who had a hard time shared that the workshop gave them added value. Both management teams decided unanimously to now introduce mindfulness across the board to all employees who choose to take part.

But it wasn't all smooth. One of the challenges that people shared about their experience was that they found it hard to turn off their phones and devices for the sessions. Although they all did turn off their phones in the end, I would assume that most people in today's society would find it a bit uneasy to set aside the phone, even just for a few hours.

Talking about being, isn't it interesting that some people find it so hard to be quiet? To be in the present? I think this is something that we all need to think about. Mindfulness not only reduces stress, but sustained practice each day helps a person to develop other levels of personal awareness and well-being.

Over time, through personal experience and discussions with others who took part in the management workshop, I realized an important lesson. Although the workshop was amazing and incredibly beneficial, and I highly recommend it for both individuals and businesses, the key to success and personal well-being is for each individual to take responsibility to practice daily.

Practicing Mindfulness

Mindfulness trains you to be able to shift gears from a busy state of "doing" to a state of "being." It doesn't mean that we stop our life. We continue to check our email, drive, cook, and work, but in a mindful way and not just reacting on autopilot to the world around us. When we practice mindfulness, we learn to focus our attention on what is happening in the present moment, in a non-judgmental way.

With practice, we can learn to be aware of our feelings, emotions, sensations, and thoughts from moment to moment, rather than merely reacting automatically to stimuli around us. Practicing mindfulness has been proven to give people an important moment between stimuli and reaction, to consider what we don't want and focus on what we truly want.

I have been told that it has been proven that mindfulness also activates compassion networks in the brain. When people quiet their minds and focus on the present moment without judgment, they start to notice similarities between themselves and others. They begin to develop a higher level of connection between themselves and others around them. To me, this is a win-win.

Harmonious Existence in Business

There are a number of ways to look at the value of Being within the work environment. Within the *Doing Good Model*, we define this value as "harmonious existence with all of the components that create the whole," and I'd like to point out how we applied this value to the relationships between our shareholders, management teams, and unions.

First, let me say that I am extremely proud of our relationships with our unions. I think this is an exceptional way to see the outcome of a values-based vision and how it is implemented within the workplace. It is amazing to see such positive relationships in the fields of finance, real estate and infrastructure, renewable energy, and water and salt.

Across the Arison Group, there are more than a dozen unions, some of them very large, with thousands of employees. Within industry, there usually exists a natural unease between union representatives and management, because unions want the best for their members, and management is traditionally thought to always put more emphasis on productivity and profitability.

A Foundation of Trust and Respect

Caring about people and the world we live in is at the core of our *Doing Good Model*. The management teams in the various companies, both public and private, have succeeded over the years in building positive and productive relationships with the unions. It comes down to having consciously created a foundation of trust and respect. This trust and respect goes both ways, from management to the union and back from the union to the management teams.

One of the main ways they built this trust and continue to do so is to involve union representatives in all decisions that affect the workforce, and doing so before final decisions are made. Of course, there are different perspectives, and things are not always agreed upon, but I believe that having an open-door policy and truly listening to concerns and requests enables a productive relationship.

One of my chairmen recently said, "Not all decisions we make in the company are going to be ground-breaking, but you have to treat all decisions, even the small ones, carefully, because you just don't know how certain initiatives are going to be received by your workforce." Here is a case in point that happened recently at the main offices of our infrastructure and real estate company. There was space at the new facility and an interest in creating a gym room where employees could work out before or after work hours. It sounded like a very positive move, lots of people really liked the idea, and it would have been easy to approve it and get it done.

But management felt that, as always, they should speak to the union first before making this decision to see if it would be well received by the workforce at large. The majority of the workforce does not work from the main office facility but out in the field, on large construction sites in countries around the world. Many projects are being constructed in all kinds of working conditions where it would be impossible for them to have a gym.

When the union was consulted about the possibility of adding a gym room to the main offices, union reps felt that the workforce at large would view the gym room as a special perk for the managers that the vast majority of the workforce, namely the field workers, would not have access to. The final decision was made with their input and with fairness in mind: the gym room project would not proceed at that time.

A similar question arose about adding a new cafeteria within the main offices, and again the union was consulted. Similar concerns were raised that the field workers should not be slighted or treated any differently, so the cafeteria plans were not approved until it was determined that all field staff working out on construction projects would have access to an organized lunch. Once that was confirmed, the new cafeteria was approved and added for the benefit of workers at the main offices of the company.

The chairman went on to explain that since Shikun & Binui is comprised of so many unions, they all need to work together on-site and around the world. It is critical that communication is open, respectful, and trustworthy, otherwise productive work just would not get done. I believe that it all comes down to them knowing that we truly care. To me, the success of the company, and all of my companies, is very much based on the harmonious existence of all the components.

"Being" at the Mandarin Oriental Hotel

Sometimes simple decisions within a business can make a big difference to your clients or customers. I love it when I see something that speaks to me or makes me smile. When I was traveling last year, I received a very nice gesture within one of the hotel chains in which I was staying.

In this case, I came in from a long flight in the middle of the night to the Mandarin Oriental Hotel in New York and found a thoughtful message of peace and tranquility that had been left on a printed card on my pillow, inspiring me to take a moment and be in the moment.

During my stay, I found out that there was a series of these inspiring message cards. Each had its own short phrase, and the words "In recognition of our Oriental heritage, we are delighted to share with you Chinese characters and Zen-inspired practices." There were seven cards in total, each with a different message, each intended for a different day of the week: Sunday—*energy*; Monday—*relaxation*; Tuesday—*prosperity*; Wednesday—*clarity*; Thursday—*meditation*; Friday—*balance*; and Saturday—*serenity*.

I was so happy to see other businesses promoting values. I have always said that if we want to see a good world, a positive world, we each need to do our part. I try to do my part in everything that I am involved in, and it is inspiring to me when I come across others that do the same.

The card with the message that I received after a long flight inspired me to be in the moment, and with inner peace, I fell asleep. After a good night's sleep, I could get up refreshed for my meetings in the morning. This brings me to our next chapter, which goes deeper into the value of *Inner Peace*.

CHAPTER SEVEN

Inner Peace

INNER PEACE

An internal, personal, continuous, and constant process that leads us to a quiet place, balanced and tranquil within us.

Finding Tranquility Within

Inner peace is a state of being at ease with yourself and having enough awareness and understanding to keep yourself centered in the face of stress, discord, or any challenges life might throw your way. Inner peace is considered by many to be a state of consciousness or enlightenment, a sort of euphoria, but I believe it's merely an outcome of knowing yourself.

Finding inner peace comes about when we are at peace with all of our "parts," some of which we can see and some we cannot. When you think of yourself, you probably just visualize your physical body, but there are so many other layers that make up your total being. For example, we each have our unique genetics, thought processes, belief systems, emotions, feelings, and senses.

Then all these parts, whether we are conscious or unconscious of them, are connected to an energetic field that vibrates within us, around us, and extends beyond our physical bodies out into the world. Therefore, who we are and how we react is also connected to what we are absorbing or feeling through our senses and intuition from the vibrational web around us. It all forms an amazing system.

So the way to find inner peace is to see and then accept all parts of ourselves, to recognize that all of our parts are legitimate, and there is a reason that they exist. I believe that reason is so we can learn, grow, and expand as individuals and as collective humanity. Our parts are there in order to be recognized and accepted, and then one can choose what one wants for oneself. How do you want to feel? How do you want your thought process to be? What affects you? What kind of person do you want to be? Once you know yourself and have recognized all of your parts and accepted them, you can let go of what is not right for you, what is no longer needed.

Of course, I recognize that we each have aspects about ourselves that we wish we could change. But first we have to see ourselves as we truly are and learn to accept all of our layers. This means not judging yourself, not saying some parts are good and some are bad, but instead trying to see each aspect of yourself for what it is and choosing what you want and who you want to be. It's important to understand that when we judge ourselves and others, the reflection that we receive back from others is judgment as well.

So in essence, everything that we see outside of ourselves is a mirror of what we are feeling internally. If we wake up fearful each day, for example, we will draw unsettling events and unpleasant people into our sphere. But if we wake up synchronized in all aspects of ourselves, feeling positive about the day, and assume that we will have a productive and happy day, then we will draw more positive experiences and individuals our way.

This is why I believe that everything that comes into our lives is there for the sole purpose of teaching us specific lessons so we can grow and expand. While some of the things that happen to us might seem pretty intense when they are happening, if we understand the mirror and the life lesson it is trying to teach us, we can transform ourselves and, that way, transform our experiences.

Finding Peace in the Workplace

So what does Inner Peace look like within a business or organization? In other words, how can you create a quiet, balanced, and tranquil place to work? It's not as hard as you might think. In fact, you can use the same process of understanding and relating to yourself, to relate and understand those around you.

So in the same way that each human being is made up of so many different parts, so too does each human being serve as an integral part of the bigger whole within a business or organization. Once each person in a workplace comes to know and respect themselves, then they can proceed to get to know, accept, and respect each person they work with. As your work relationships grow and expand, just keep doing more of what works and discard what is not productive within that workplace. In this way, gradually your own sense of inner peace and well-being will permeate to others, and the workplace itself will be more peaceful and harmonious.

Remember, you cannot change anyone else. You can't make anyone else be at peace with themselves. But the good news is that you can set an example. One of the best ways to get those around you engaged in a collective journey toward inner peace is for you to model peace within yourself, acceptance and respect, first for yourself and then for the others around you.

Essence of Life

I have always believed that in order to achieve peace in the world, we each need to achieve peace within ourselves and our surroundings. It was with this vision in mind that I established the Essence of Life philanthropic organization.

Essence of Life has evolved greatly through the years, as our collective consciousness has. In fact, one of the missions of Essence of Life at the very beginning was to heighten the collective consciousness, and it's amazing to see how far the world has come. I remember in the very beginning, when I talked of Inner Peace, people laughed at me, were cynical, and could not understand this simple concept.

People tend to think that peace is something on the outside that governments need to take care of. It is important to understand that if, one by one, people are at peace with themselves, the circles will grow, and by adding more and more individuals into the collective, eventually there will be peace on Earth. It will be a *real* peace, not a peace of negotiations or contracts that later can be broken, but a real and truthful peace that comes from one's inner core.

What we did at Essence of Life in order to translate this vision in a practical way was to give workshops with tools for Inner Peace. For a long time, we had a children's show that thousands of children saw, teaching them the value of Inner Peace in an entertaining way. Storytellers went out to schools to teach children through a storyline how to quiet themselves through meditation in a very simple way. We created school programs that showed children the way to connect to themselves and be aware of their feelings and how they are acting.

Today, Essence of Life primarily shares the values of Inner Peace through our interactive visitor's center in Israel for children and their parents or teachers. We also have a radio station (in Hebrew at this time) that gives a different perspective on all issues concerning all circles of life. Looking at an issue as a tool to better ourselves creates within ourselves the kind of future we all want to see. The station also promotes inner peace through its choice of music and by presenting practical ways that listeners can strive more toward their own inner peace.

We have an Internet site that is constantly being updated to be aligned with the general consciousness. Today, I believe that even though most people don't know how to reach inner peace, they do understand the concept, and there are many people who are pursuing the path.

Essence of Life was the motivation behind the value of Inner Peace in the *Doing Good Model*. As I said, in order to reach world peace, we each need to reach peace within ourselves and our surroundings, and by furthering this value in the model, we are growing the circles of awareness, giving tools, so that step by step, people understand that if we want world peace, we each need to take personal responsibility for our own inner peace and resonate that outward.

Jill Bolte Taylor's Stroke of Insight

I became aware of brain scientist Jill Bolte Taylor and of the incredible experience she lived through by watching a TED Talk presentation that she gave. In her speech, she described how she suffered a massive stroke, and how she began to realize that her various brain functions were shutting down, one after the other, including her ability to move, her speech, and her awareness of herself.[1]

---

[1] http://www.ted.com/talks/jill_bolte_taylor_s_powerful_stroke_of_insight?language=en#

After the amazement of finding herself still alive after the stroke, Taylor spent the next eight years recovering her abilities to think, walk, and talk. She has since become a powerful spokesperson for stroke recovery and for the possibility of coming back from a brain injury stronger than before. Today, she is a truly inspirational speaker and author who travels on behalf of the Harvard Brain Tissue Resource Center.

In Taylor's case, although the stroke damaged the left side of her brain, her recovery unleashed a torrent of creative energy from the right side of her brain. It was an incredible experience for Taylor to learn what life is like when your left brain isn't working and you don't have any linear thinking, critical reasoning, or judgments of any kind, of yourself or others. During part of her healing experience, she merely existed.

But following her stroke, she lived through it all firsthand. She tells about what happened to her in such crystal-clear terms. I was fascinated to hear how she described it. "To use a powerful metaphor, we have two magnificent information-processing machines inside our heads," she explains. "Our right mind focuses on our similarities, the present moment, inflection of voice, and the bigger picture of how we are all connected. Because it focuses on our similarities, in my mind [the right side of the brain] is compassionate, expansive, open, and supportive of others.

"Juxtaposed to that, our left brain thinks linearly, creates and understands language, defines the boundaries of where we begin and where we end, judges what is right and wrong, and is a master of details, details, and more details about those details. Because it focuses on our differences and specializes in critical judgment of those unlike ourselves, our left brain character tends to be our source of bigotry, prejudice, and fear or hate of the unfamiliar."[2]

It was an incredible experience for Taylor to learn what life is like without any linear thinking, without any judgments of any kind of herself or others. She merely existed, and she realized that we do have the power as humans to choose to be kind over being judgmental, and we do have the power to be open rather than stuck in our fear.

Taylor makes the point that because we know so much more about how our brains work than we ever have before, we now are able to actually direct our own evolution. As she puts it, "We know we have the ability to not only experience our biological circuitry, but to observe it, nurture it, and change it. We have the ability to consciously choose who and how we want to be in the world."[3]

I totally agree that each and every one of us has the power to choose who and how we want to be in the world. Keeping that in mind, I passionately believe that finding inner peace individually is the key to achieving world peace collectively.

From *Inner Peace* to *Fulfillment*, the *Doing Good Model* expands.

---

[2] http://www.huffingtonpost.com/dr-jill-bolte-taylor/neuroscience_b _2404554.html
[3] Ibid.

CHAPTER EIGHT

Fulfillment

FULFILLMENT

*Realizing the self's full potential (while being
at peace with our choices).*

The Highway of Life

Reaching one's fulfillment is like taking a highway. There are many paths, side roads, winding roads, roads that take you where you want to be, and others that get you lost. There are so many paths to choose from. Let me describe it.

In my mind's eye, I see a movie theater with many different movies to choose from. There are scary movies, dramas, thrillers, action flicks, comedies, and romances. There's even science fiction. To me, this basically describes our lives. We can choose the movie we want to go into and we can choose the path we want to take.

In my personal life, I have taken many roads and seen many movies. It has taken a long process of inner connection, but I now believe that I am on my personal highway of fulfillment. It's funny how you can be fulfilled in your career and not personally. Or quite the opposite: you might be fulfilled personally but not in your work. There are many types of fulfillment: self-fulfillment, interpersonal fulfillment, family fulfillment, and career fulfillment. Each person can look for themselves where they feel fulfilled and where they don't.

Fulfillment is a personal introspective, and what we see on the outside is not necessarily the truth. A person can seem extremely successful, having money, position, family, and more, and still feel that something is missing, still feel unfulfilled. So fulfillment is very individual. People tend to think in general that famous people like movie stars or rock stars have glamorous lifestyles, having and doing as they please, and yet, some of those people are lost and lonely, spending endless nights in hotel rooms alone or with people who don't matter, chasing what seems to be a dream instead of connecting to what is really fulfilling for them.

Seeking Fulfillment Individually and Collectively

While the path to fulfillment is different for everyone, there are a number of common desires that most people want. Regardless of your situation, where you live, your career direction, or your life path, I believe everyone feels a will to expand their awareness and knowledge, and to grow generally as human beings. We all want to feel worthy and valuable, healthy, and at peace. We all want to feel connected and part of something.

We all want good energy in our homes and in our workplaces, and to be part of a group of positive people who are making a difference. Although I own my businesses, and technically, I can just demand what I want, I understand that in order to create that kind of good energy that I want in my group, it has to come from a pure intention, personal example, and creating the kind of environment that is conducive to that kind of fulfillment. Fulfillment is internal and personal; it is not something you can dictate to others.

That is why I try to create the kind of place where people feel supported and valued, where they can contribute their talents and feel they are an important part of the collective. Each person has a place, above and beyond their job, to connect to what they are most passionate about. I believe that this is the way to lead a workforce that is creative, productive, and engaged—a group of people that can really make a difference for themselves individually, for their families, and for the companies they work in.

Being fulfilled means that you are happy and alive, realizing your full potential. Just as there are many different paths and so many types of movies, there are endless ways that people can feel fulfilled; everyone is different. Every day we make choices, and an important part of being fulfilled is being at peace with the choices we make. Fulfillment is found when you find a balance between your choices and accepting their outcomes.

Finding What Makes You Fulfilled

For each of us as individuals, finding our life purpose is about our personal vision. To find what makes you fulfilled, you could begin by sitting quietly and thinking about what makes you feel fulfilled. What times in your life did you feel the most alive, happy, and passionate? What makes you lose track of time? What activity makes you feel so full of energy that you could just go on and on?

This sounds simple, but give yourself time to truly think about it. As you find a place deep within yourself, think about what you truly love to do. Not what is expected of you, not what you expect of yourself, not what anyone else thinks, but what you truly want for yourself in life, what makes your heart sing.

I have found that connecting to what makes me happy resonates outward to the rest of my life, putting everything else that I do in a more positive light, a more fulfilling light. As you connect to your own innermost passions and fulfill them, I believe you will feel stronger and happier inside, and you might begin to see all the possibilities that are out there for you.

Finding Fulfillment in Your Career

To reach fulfillment at an organizational level, I believe that it takes a higher purpose, something that drives you individually and collectively each day to strive for something better, something bigger than ourselves. We can see through history that those who had vision, persistence, and passion and cared about something higher than themselves, cared about people and the betterment of our collective future, are the people and the organizations that created true and long-lasting transformation.

It all comes down, in my opinion, to values. It's not enough to create the best product, or give the highest level of service, unless underneath it all, you really care about people and the community you work in. True values go above and beyond a vision statement, a mission statement, something that is on the wall but no one really connects to it or works according to it. True values need to be implemented in all levels of business, connecting all employees and outward, to all the circles of impact that your business touches.

When values are aligned with the personal and the organizational in a way that is clear, focused, and engaging, that's when the individual and the collective can both prosper and be fulfilled.

Although being profitable is, needless to say, an important outcome of any business, I believe that vision and mission is something that is above and beyond monetary profits. So if you are an owner or leading a company or organization, ask yourself, "Is our main mission being fulfilled?"

Being an employee, do you feel excited to go to work? Do you feel part of something big? Something important? If employees are feeling part of a bigger picture, and the owners are achieving their mission, I believe there is then an alignment of personal and organizational fulfillment.

My *Personal* Story of Fulfillment:
Material for Thought

I recently came out with a book, *Material for Thought*. This book is about my personal growth process through art. The book includes most of my artwork, oil paintings, sketches, sculptures, photography, and more. I love my book! I wrote it for myself, created it for myself, and like I said, I love it! This for me is true fulfillment. It's funny, I have basically been creating my whole life, but I never felt fulfilled.

Since I was raised in a business environment, I was brought up partly to believe that if you are not productive in business, then you don't have very much value. Although most of the individuals in my family were creative people and some supported the arts through philanthropy, nobody in my family really sought out personal fulfillment as an artist because the mindset was it wasn't a good enough career. That's not where the money is. For me, this was an underlying challenge my whole life.

For me personally, the expression of art was at the innermost core of my being, and I always felt that my essence was that of an artist, of a creator. But being that I felt conditioned to be focused on business and success, it was very hard for me to express my artistic side for most of my life.

Over the years, I was fortunate to be able to use my own creative process within many of the projects I was working on. Building buildings through philanthropy, I used the opportunity to include my vision for design, working with architects, choosing colors and materials, and giving birth to building after building, project after project, using my passion.

In business and philanthropy, with others at my side, I used my creative insight to instill real change, which includes transforming several existing companies and organizations that are part of the Arison Group. I also put my creative energy into vision while building a new company and several more philanthropic organizations.

Although I used my artistic soul in business and philanthropy, it never gave me true fulfillment, fulfillment at the deepest, most intimate level. I always wanted to create art but I could never imagine in my wildest dreams that I could become an artist. I always felt some kind of inner barrier that didn't allow me to express myself through art. I always felt that I wasn't good enough. I compared myself to other people, and I was always looking from the outside in rather than from the inside out.

I finally overcame the barriers and allowed myself the joyful experience of getting back into creating art, just for myself, for the love of it. I was finally able to connect to my inner core and bring my creative soul out into my artwork. Once I was painting and creating artistic works again and began compiling those art pieces into a book, I then found that everything in my life became more fulfilling.

To me, my art book is the manifestation of my creative soul, one that is intimate, deep, and from within. I came to a place where I was generally happy and enjoyed most aspects of my life, but after tapping into and reaching my own true fulfillment, all of a sudden, all parts of my life—businesses, philanthropy, relationships—everything became better, everything had more meaning. I feel that finally my whole life is now connected to my innermost passion, and that has literally transformed everything for me.

If you don't already find a deep level of personal fulfillment with your own work, keep seeking that which will make you whole, but remember that wholeness is from within. Once you find it, what truly fulfills you, I believe that you will find a way to enhance your career and revitalize your personal life. Fulfillment has the power to transform all levels of your existence in the most miraculous way.

Individual Fulfillment: The Desert Talks

Striving for personal fulfillment can be accomplished in so many different ways. I recently heard a great story about one of our senior engineers named Noam. He enjoys his daily work at Salt of the Earth working at our Eilat location, but he also has found highly fulfilling outlets for his own creative talents outside of work.

Photography is Noam's hobby and his passion, and he delights in finding the beauty in everyday scenes. Seeking a way to support his community, he found great satisfaction and fulfillment in volunteering to share his expertise with students at a local school, working with young people with special needs who were keen to learn photography.

Noam showed them how to use a camera and how to find beauty in everyday objects and scenes that they saw at their school grounds and in their daily lives. Creating their own images and displaying their photographic artwork for their teachers and parents was a wonderful outlet for these students to express their own identity in a concrete way and build their self-confidence and pride in what they could do.

Noam also worked on his own project, which filled his heart and soul with joy. Over a period of years, he went out into the desert at different times of day with his camera to capture many different scenes from various angles, under natural light at dawn, midday, and dusk, to create the most beautiful and thought-provoking images he could.

The project eventually turned into a labor of love when he selected the best shots from his thousands of images and self-published his own book of photographic artwork, called *Desert Dessert—The Desert Talks.* Throughout the book, he added a value, one or two words, that he felt represented each photograph. It took endless hours and considerable resources to complete the book, but he loved the process of creation, and it now stands as a unique celebration of natural beauty.

Community Fulfillment: ArtPort TelAviv

My son Jason Arison has chosen to focus his professional work within the philanthropic side of the Arison Group. Being chairman of The Ted Arison Family Foundation, he oversees the many aspects of operations, including several philanthropic organizations, management, funding, community collaborations, and the other needs of the community that arise. This work could be fulfilling in its own right, but like all of us, Jason wanted to express his own passion for the arts in his own way.

"I always felt a strong personal connection to art and music, and I wanted to build something from the ground up, something just for artists," he says. "It was something I wanted to do for many, many years. I was inspired by my grandfather and his wife, my Grandma Linnie, who supported young artists in the United States, and I wanted to do that too, but in my own way."

His vision manifested through his founding of the Center for Young Art, and within that entity, he established ArtPort TelAviv. He researched various models of residency art programs around the world for more than a year to determine the best structure. His goal was to set up ArtPort to support emerging artists by giving them studio space and a supportive environment where they could advance their skills and experience in creating art.

He knew that even highly talented artists can struggle to establish a career in which they will be most fulfilled. Instead, some have to accept work that they do not find fulfilling, a "day job" they might not really enjoy, just to pay the bills. Then they struggle to find extra time and resources to do their art only on a part-time or casual basis.

However, the ArtPort program gives artists (both Israeli and visiting international artists) a chance to be supported while they create new works and establish their own independent and sustainable careers in the art world. Artists can make an application to be part of the program, and a committee of outside members, who are highly respected professional artists and leading curators from the art world, select the best candidates.

Being able to do what one truly loves to do as a full-time job is tremendously fulfilling. So far, in only a few years since its inception, twenty-five individual artists have been supported through the program.

While the artists are in residency at ArtPort for one year, they have access to a studio for their use, accommodation if needed, and a monthly scholarship, and they participate in a professional enrichment program. This includes workshops, lectures, discussions with peers and industry leaders, exhibition opportunities, collaborative partnerships, and professional exposure through web and studio visits. While receiving all of these benefits, each artist commits to creating a community project, integrating their art into society in a meaningful way.

In this way, under Jason's vision and leadership, ArtPort has become a home for emerging artists, a dynamic environment, and a place that will be reflected upon as a turning point in the lives of these talented people. It is a nurturing platform for them to grow into the full professional artists they wish to become. While it is still new and growing, it is becoming an internationally respected program, and Jason himself was acknowledged in the Forbes Israel newspaper as one of the top ten people influencing the local art scene.

I can see the heart that Jason puts into the many aspects of the program, choosing the right people to have everything run smoothly. But I also see the true fulfillment on his face whenever I happen to be at an ArtPort event, exhibition, or community project. This is when I see Jason in his true element. I can see the light and joy shining through his eyes.

Jason's excitement continues as the artist's careers take off. "When I see our artists move on from the ArtPort program to qualify for other prestigious programs around the world, or when they sell their art to museums or galleries, I feel so incredibly happy and fulfilled. It's an amazing feeling."

The Different Paths of Fulfillment

It is important for me to note that although these examples have been from the art world, fulfillment is different for each individual. For some it's art, for others it's nature, and of course, just as there are countless people in the world, that's how many paths of fulfillment there can be. Each person needs to tap into their innermost place and find what is fulfilling to them.

When we find true fulfillment at home, at work, and in all circles of our lives, we become whole. Being whole powerfully resonates outward and serves as a positive example to others of what can be achieved. I added *Fulfillment* intuitively to the *Doing Good Model*, understanding its importance. Each value has a role to play in the bigger picture of the whole model, and equally important is our next value: *Vitality*.

CHAPTER NINE

Vitality

VITALITY

An internal, driving energy that enables a dynamic pace of life, vibrancy, and constant renewal.

Discovering Your Spark

Vitality is the spark inside yourself that you can feel; it is a pulse, a vibration, the feeling of being alive. Vitality is what lets you experience joy in life, by being thankful for just waking up in the morning, smelling the flowers, and enjoying a cup of coffee with a friend.

Feeling vital is different for everyone. For some of us, including myself, diet, exercise, and meditation are important parts of feeling vital. For others, it's starting the day by listening to music, and for others, it's vital for their vitality to enjoy what they do at work. So it's not about a certain diet, and there is not one single solution that works for everyone. Just be aware of what you makes you feel vital, knowing that your mind and body will tell you what it is that gives you vitality and what you need to feel most vibrant and alive.

Within a company or organization, vitality is very much the same thing. Entities that are successful have a "pulse" that can be felt, an energy that drives the company and its employees forward. A company with a good pulse is welcoming to employees, and that is especially amplified when employees are coming to work with an inner vitality of their own. What could be better than employing people who wake up with a positive emotion and a healthy spark and who love what they do each day in their career? But we shouldn't take that for granted.

To have that in your employees, you need to create the kind of environment that promotes well-being. Of course, to reach a collective vitality, each person needs to take responsibility for their own vitality.

For me, Vitality is a value that connects deep within myself. It is a state of mind and body that I personally need to take a look at and connect to on a daily basis. We face challenges in all circles of our lives. It is easy to fall into a mundane existence, and it is our individual responsibility to choose vitality every day.

There is a lot more to vitality than meets the eyes. Within each of the companies, I sought to instill a sense of vitality and life. These companies seemed to have no real vision beyond day-to-day operational concerns, so I made it my purpose to connect each of them to the bigger picture, looking beyond the bottom line to the value and vitality they could bring to themselves and the world.

We have seen so many positive outcomes of introducing and promoting the value of Vitality within our companies. We have seen that vitality boosts productivity and achievement. It fuels innovation, initiative, and engagement, making people want to strive for a better life of their own, a better way to do things in the companies that keeps everyone feeling vital and alive.

The Vitality forum actually sprouted from the employees who were interested in implementing this value across the board in all of our business companies and philanthropic organizations. After creating a number of initiatives, I was approached by management and some of the employees on how I see further implementation of the value of Vitality.

My response was clear. Vitality is different for everyone. For me, when I dance, I feel the most vital. But for each individual, what makes them tick is something deep and intimate that only they can say. Therefore, I recommended that we ask the employees what makes them feel vital, and that they share with us how they would suggest implementation in the workplace. It was amazing to see the results of the survey and the enthusiasm it created.

Salt of the Earth and Vitality

The value of Vitality originally came from the vision of Salt of the Earth. While brainstorming together with Arison Investments and the Salt of the Earth management teams, I noted the fact that in order to live we need salt. Our bodies need salt.

While talking about the importance of salt, I found it amazing when one of our managers showed me a list of quotes from the Bible. It turns out that the Bible is full of quotes on salt. That is when I realized the importance of salt and how vital it is in our lives. The vision of the salt company, Vitality, was born. The value of Vitality was born.

Our company, Salt of the Earth, is the principal manufacturer of salt in Israel, and our products are marketed to both industrial and retail customers in Israel and abroad. The workings of our salt company relate directly to Vitality, in that the salt operations reflect the dynamic pace of life and constant renewal.

At two large operations, Salt of the Earth extracts salt by taking naturally occurring salt water and turning it into salt crystals through evaporation in a series of salt ponds. While this is based on ancient techniques, our operations today are highly technical, fully sustainable, and environmentally friendly, vital in every sense of the word.

The fact is that the human body needs salt to live. Yet the reputation of salt has become a negative over the years. There are people who claim too much salt is unhealthy, but without salt in our diets we would perish. Not only that, salt gave the human race an ability to preserve food, making it hugely important to our development.

Human civilization and ancient trading routes were greatly influenced by the availability of salt. Salt was so valuable that it was even used as a form of currency by numerous people. It is commonly believed that Roman soldiers were paid with salt at certain times, which led to the common expression that someone who did their job well was "worth their salt." Even our modern word "salary" is derived from the Latin word *salārium*, which means "payment in salt." The word "salt" is used in various contexts in the Bible as a metaphor for permanence, fidelity, loyalty, usefulness, and purification. Salt is also referenced as a covenant of friendship and compassion.

Today, I am proud to say that the vitality that has been created by the management and employees in our salt company has introduced a pulse and an aliveness. Driven by innovation and sustainability, they have fully embraced the values under the *Doing Good Model*.

While the workforce at Salt of the Earth is only just over a hundred people in total, they have been a big part of our cross-organizational transformation. I am amazed at their resourcefulness, and I love seeing what they have done within the company, embracing their own natural vitality.

Introducing Vitality at the Arison Group Headquarters

Arison Group employees at our head offices found their own ways to promote this value when they set out to create their own projects to celebrate vitality in ways that were most meaningful to them.

Our spokesperson for the company, who also does media relations in Israel for the Arison Group, helped establish the Vitality forum halfway through 2013 because there were many people at the office interested in this value. The group decided to host regular lectures and workshops on nutrition, health, and exercise. Outside speakers have come in to present on Meatless Monday, for example, and the value of incorporating a regular exercise routine into one's life.

From these initiatives, the group decided to develop a book featuring recipes for employees' favorite healthy dishes. Creative and fun photos were taken of the employees interacting with food to reinforce the positive messages. These images were published on the back of each of the individual colorful recipe cards that ultimately made up the *Arison Group Recipe Book*.

Since then, other businesses and organizations within the group have become interested and started their own initiatives to reinforce vitality and wellness at their own offices, wherever they might be. For example, at the infrastructure and real estate company, the employees chose to organize group games and activities after work to promote wellness and vitality. Once Shikun & Binui tried this fun and successful initiative, more of our companies and offices within the Arison Group wanted to follow suit and try it too, which they did.

As a result, within just a short time, Vitality has proven to be alive and well, living and breathing within our organization, not just at Salt of the Earth, where it began, but any place where employees are making positive and life-affirming choices about their workplace, individual vitality, and the vitality of the company at large.

The Rise of Running

As children, so many of us were raised playing outside with our friends, running and jumping whenever we would get the chance. The sheer joy of the movement of our bodies is being rediscovered by adults in the form of running clubs and individual running routines that continue to keep us feeling vibrant and alive.

I think that running has become such a popular activity because it can be woven into our busy lives in a relatively easy way. You don't have to be an elite athlete to run, and you don't need expensive equipment to get started. For those of us who tend to lead driven lives, running is an activity that is easily measurable and for which you can set personal goals that are attainable.

Beyond just taking an early morning run, marathon running has enjoyed a huge resurgence in popularity around the world. Dating back to ancient times, the word "marathon" is based on the legendary run taken by the Greek soldier Pheidippides when he was a messenger going from the Battle of Marathon to Athens. Today, a marathon is a long-distance road race with an official distance of just over 26 miles (42.12 kilometers).

Today, marathon races are organized around the world with most of the competitors being recreational athletes who train to participate. In the United States alone in 2013, more than 1,000 full-length marathon races were held, and according to Running USA's annual Marathon Report, just over

500,000 runners completed those races. Many of these were held in smaller centers, but for the larger and most prestigious races, runners may choose to travel across the country and across oceans to participate.

You may choose to run for yourself or compete in a marathon, but regardless of your goals, once you get started in a running routine, you'll probably feel the health benefits almost immediately. A steady running routine or one that involves a brisk walk each day is hugely transformative for most people. Getting out and moving very often leads to a path to better cardiovascular health, wiser choices in diet, better sleep patterns, increased energy levels, a feeling of overall vitality, and so much more.

The value of *Vitality* cannot be overstated, and I believe it is something that our bodies naturally crave. Vitality breathes life into our personal and business lives, serving as that internal driving energy that enables a dynamic pace of life with whatever we are doing. From this point, we move beyond the personal internal values to the values that invite us to interact more with the world around us, starting with the value of *Giving*.

Activate Your Goodness While Attaining Win-Win

CHAPTER TEN

Giving

GIVING

To give from a sincere, empowering, and true place.

The Value of Giving

The truth is that giving is one of the most powerful things that we can do. I always say that even a smile that brightens someone else's day is a gift that you are giving. People think that in order to give, you need to have a lot: wealth, position, something of monetary value. But for me, giving starts from even the simplest acts of kindness: a listening ear, a hug, a small gesture that can change another person's day.

It is important to give in an authentic way, a way that is balanced, that you yourself feel good about; then you gain just as much as the person or the cause you are giving to. The result of giving without consideration for yourself is depleting, and yet giving with consideration to yourself is uplifting and powerful.

The Different Faces of Giving

Giving and Volunteering are very closely related values, but for the purpose of the *Doing Good Model*, it was important to me that they be stated individually. Each component in the model has its own individuality, and yet together, they become whole. Although originally management grouped Giving and Volunteering together in one forum, it is quite interesting to see that now, after a couple of years, the employees themselves came to the conclusion that although they are related, they are quite different at the core. Now we have one forum for Giving and a different forum for Volunteering.

Giving can be volunteering, which is giving of your time. But giving is so much broader. Think of all the ways you can give: you can donate money; you can give advice, mentorship, friendship; and so much more.

I believe gratitude is also an important face to giving. First and foremost, gratitude to oneself for the caring, one's will, and the capabilities of the gifts that one gives. Gratitude to the organization that you are part of that is giving, whether it is inward for the benefit of their employees or outward to the benefit of the community they work in. Gratitude in the form of a reflection coming back from the recipients who can appreciate the gifts they are receiving. In general, I believe *gratitude* is an essential part of giving.

Business and Philanthropy: The Giving Forum

Although we have given a lot of donations over the years through our family foundation and through corporate giving within all our businesses, we are still exploring the value of Giving through the Giving forum. We feel that it is important that we all have a common understanding about the values if we are intending to live them daily.

For example, I recently attended a forum meeting where we had a deep discussion about the value of Giving. Someone said that giving should be done unconditionally, and I said to them, basically there is no such thing as unconditional giving, and I would advise them not to use that phrase. Let me explain myself. As the definition of this value states: to give from a sincere, empowering, and true place, *a true place*—how can it be unconditional? Every organization has a strategy that means that they give according to their vision and heart's desire. That in itself is already *conditional.*

This means that when giving to a cause, one expects to see specific outcomes. If you give advice or expertise in an effort to help someone, you might expect that person to listen, and you would hope that some good might come out of your efforts, some tangible results for the person or cause you wish to support. Indeed, if you had no expectations at all, no boundaries, and no vision, what outcome *could* you really expect?

Whether you are a foundation or a company, it is important to determine a strategy for your giving so that you can create the impact that you are trying to achieve. In general, organizations that give to the community are doing so in order to create positive change, and that is the outcome they want to see.

I feel strongly that when you give, you do need to have boundaries. When you give without boundaries, you become a victim. Even if you give a hug, you wouldn't want to be slapped in return. A non-profit organization or a corporation that gives to a cause expects their donation to be used as intended.

Please let me explain myself further, because I am not talking about giving with the expectation that if I give something to you, you will give something back to me, or you will owe me. But even as an individual who is giving to someone else, that person expects gratitude in return and proper use of the gift. For example, if you give a friend money for a specific purpose, such as to pay off a debt they owe, and instead they go to Las Vegas and gambles it all away, that was not your intention for the gift you gave. That is what I mean when I say that no gift is truly unconditional at this stage in our evolution.

However, as we continue to grow and evolve, I believe we are going forward to a place that love and giving will be unconditional. But that takes growth, a higher perspective, and the understanding that when you give unconditionally, you have to let go and be at peace with the outcome, whatever that may be.

Giving from the Heart

One of my very best friends has shown me over the years that giving has nothing to do with money. As Mother Teresa said,

"It's not how much we give, but how much love we put into giving." My friend and I have always been very close and our children grew up together. Over the years, I became wealthy, but she often struggled when it came to money. However, being the large heart that she is, she never had scarcity when it came to giving love.

Being the kind of person that she is, and the two of us always talking and sharing about how we can make a difference in the world and give, each one in her own way, my friend decided to be a foster parent so she could give children love, a home, and a better future. The apple doesn't fall far from the tree. Her youngest daughter, from the time I knew her as a young child, always wanted to help the less fortunate. She has since spent years in Haiti after the earthquake and even risked her life to help children in Ebola-affected Sierra Leone, Africa.

I always say that in order to do good for others, you need to do good for yourself, but I also say that the best way to give is to connect to your passion. That's what my friend and her daughter did and continue to do. Heidi Wills says, "A good person is a gift to the whole world."

Back to Business: A Vehicle for Corporate Giving

I have always believed that business has an important role in giving back to the community. It goes without saying that philanthropic organizations give, and that is their essence. But in business, the old-school belief was only to care about the bottom line, while today, the new-school understanding is that every business is part of a community, part of a country, and part of our planet. Therefore, every business has the responsibility to do their part.

I talked a little bit about Matan, an organization that I created under the international United Way model. These organizations help companies both on a corporate level and an employee level to give according to their corporate giving strategy and the knowledge of what's needed.

Implementing Matan in Bank Hapoalim many years ago was an incredible experience. It proved to me what I always believed, that business is part of a community, and it has a place in making a difference by giving back to that community. I always knew in my heart that employee motivation, excitement, and creativity grows when people are a part of something greater than the daily business. People want to make a difference and they want to contribute, but they don't always know how. When you show them the way, they come on board passionately.

Through a vehicle like Matan or United Way, the corporation can give matching funds to employee funds that are being raised. Employees can give according to their heart's desire, whether it is the same causes as the company chooses or something totally different that is closer to their hearts. It can be a one-time donation or an ongoing gift. Employees can donate out of their salaries, which can be taken out, in many cases, automatically, or they can donate from their vacation time or bonuses if received. There are many ways and styles to give, and all of them are valuable.

Matan has shown the way to many more companies of all sizes how to give, each one according to what's right for them. Over the years, Bank Hapoalim has become the leader in corporate giving in Israel. All of our Arison Group companies—private, public, and non-profit—give in all circles that we work in, all over the world. It is amazing to see how the vehicle that Matan provides has truly changed the culture of giving in Israel. I experienced the same kind of motivational impact years ago, being involved with United Way in the United States.

Regardless, no matter what vehicle you use to organize your corporate giving, it is imperative to understand that you are part of a larger picture, and the impact that you have, be it big or small, is extremely important. *Volunteering* is another way to be a part of that impact, and our next chapter explores how.

So if you focus on caring for your fellow man, your surroundings, and your environment, together people, organizations, and businesses around the world can truly be part of a greater gift. The gift of a better future for us all.

CHAPTER ELEVEN

Volunteering

VOLUNTEERING

Action in the community, based on inner strength and love for others.

Follow Your Passion

The most motivated volunteers are the ones with passion for the cause. They enter a non-profit group ready and willing to make a commitment on a regular and consistent basis. Volunteers might be there once a week for two hours, or a morning twice a month, for example, helping with a cause, a group of people, or a specific project, such as meeting the extra needs of a hospital, a kindergarten, or a social service group.

Each volunteer makes a personal commitment so that the people being helped or the non-profit organization can come to count on them. The gift of their time and attention is hugely valuable, and many non-profits rely greatly on the kindness of volunteers to help them achieve their overall mission and goals. The volunteers enjoy showing up for their shift because they know someone is expecting them, and the tasks or assistance they are volunteering to do are vital to the person in need, the cause, or both.

Because of the importance for consistency of effort, not everyone can commit to be a volunteer. There was a cause in Israel that I heard about and would have loved to be part of. I looked into volunteering for that specific cause that I deeply connected to. They needed people to help hold and nurture very small infants with disabilities who had been abandoned. I felt passionate about becoming a volunteer, but you had to be there a specific number of times a week and never miss your shift, because these tiny babies counted on the touch and feel of the same people being with them so that the child could bond, feeling security, comfort, and consistency.

Since I travel internationally for both my business and philanthropic endeavors, I could not make the commitment that was necessary, but I am glad that there are people who can do so, because I believe that in order to volunteer you need a level of responsibility and commitment to those to whom you have promised your time. Although I could not commit to that specific cause, I spend my time giving and creating change in everything that I do.

There are many volunteer opportunities and they come in all shapes and sizes. Not all volunteer activities are as intensely personal or require such a high level of commitment as tending to tiny newborn babies. There is a matching cause out there for just about anyone who truly wishes to give their time.

The key is to find something you are passionate about, and connect to a person or group who needs your time and talents.

In the Workforce

What management can do is encourage volunteerism and actively support the efforts of employees who wish to do community work. In my companies, it is important to me that our employees truly choose to get involved, acting from their hearts, because they are passionate about the cause. I don't want them to sign up just because they think it's a mandated aspect of their work or because they feel they will be judged.

Our definition of Volunteering is taking "action in the community, based on inner strength and love for others," so that is what I wish people would connect to if they choose. We as leaders, I believe, should inspire, encourage, and show the way and respect personal choices.

As for me, I try to think of ways I can help or encourage our people to make the choice to volunteer from within themselves, because then they will *own* it. Once they are connected and feeling good about their commitments, they will be far more likely to enjoy themselves and keep on consistently helping with that group of seniors, children, arts enthusiasts, animals, the environment, or the overall cause, whatever it might be.

As a leader of a group, I also try to encourage my companies to give their time in the subject that they have the most knowledge about. For example, bank employees can donate their time helping people by giving them the knowledge and tools to reach their own financial freedom. Employees of the real estate and infrastructure company can give their time helping in construction, and it can be as simple as building a ramp for a person in a wheelchair.

There are so many ideas that can arise if each company or philanthropic organization looks within themselves; just as I recommended to individuals to seek out the kind of inner strength that they can give to others, so can companies. Of course, there are many employees who wish to give their time with something totally unrelated to their work, and that is a blessing as well.

Volunteering from the Heart

Community involvement strengthens social ties and it is a great way to connect to people who have common interests to your own. Volunteering promotes caring, which is a very important human value that we sometimes forget, given our busy lives and the hectic world that we live in.

Helping others in need is a great way to feel good about yourself. I know a lot of people who have fun getting in shape, training, and being part of a charity run, which keeps you fit and lets you raise awareness at the same time. There have even been studies that show that volunteering can improve your physical and psychological health.

Volunteers very often have the chance to try new skills when they volunteer, and then those talents add to their own skill set. This is an important addition to a resume because it shows a well-rounded person. Personally, when I interview someone to be a director representing me in one of my companies, along with their professional skills, I always look at the person's set of values and if they give back to the community in some way.

In today's world, you can volunteer from just about anywhere in the world that you live. Volunteer opportunities are happening just down the street in your community, at your workplace, your community center, and increasingly online. If you travel a lot, there are always causes you can connect to in any country that you visit. You or members of your workforce may have skills that are in demand in developing countries. So you can use your time, whether it is backed by your company or your own free time, to put your skills to work abroad on a special service project that is needed among any specific people or country.

I have seen the positive energy, happiness, and enthusiasm that is created in my workforce by employees who are volunteering or connected to a cause, and they say they feel proud to work in a group that supports and encourages their contributions.

A funny thing happened to me right after I was talking to my editor on the phone going through this chapter on volunteering. I was called away and needed to rush out to a meeting outside my office. I went to another office building, and when I came out of my meeting, in the elevator on the way down, there was a husband and wife talking. The woman said to her husband, "Isn't it amazing that the doctor goes to

Africa every six months and volunteers his time to perform surgery?" She went on say, "Do you know he's an eye doctor?" I smiled to myself as I was walking out of the elevator, thinking about what a coincidence it was that I was just writing about volunteering. So you see, as I said, one can volunteer basically anywhere in the world, according to one's talents, passions, and time.

Making the Right Match

I am thrilled with an organization that I took under my wing called Ruach Tova, whose name translates as "Good Spirit." When I was approached to give the original seed money and office space to get this organization going, I loved the idea of not only matching volunteers to organizations, but also matching people to people, as simple as a hairdresser giving a free haircut to someone who can't afford it.

Ruach Tova developed experience and a wide range of connections to be able to match people with the right kind of volunteer opportunity for them. It very quickly became the major connector of volunteers and organizations who need volunteers in Israel. With time and the great success of Ruach Tova, we officially adopted them to be part of our group under The Ted Arison Family Foundation.

Soon social service agencies all across the country registered with the organization through the Internet, as did many traditional and diverse non-profit organizations, which rely on volunteers to accomplish their missions and get things done.

The approach at Ruach Tova is that everyone can be included, so they have been very creative at finding placements for anyone who truly wants to volunteer. For example, if a volunteer has a disability of some kind, Ruach Tova seeks a way that technology could perhaps help that person volunteer.

Maybe you only have one day you can volunteer, and if so, they will help you make the best of it, matching you with a cause you can impact even if it is just one day. Their theory is that one day is better than none, and while some volunteers just do the one day and it's done, other people catch the good feeling and choose to continue volunteering in the future.

One day during my morning exercise, I had the vision that every person could do a good deed, be it big or small, because, as I say, even a smile that brightens someone's day is a good deed. I wanted to encourage people to do a good deed, each according to their heart's desire, and understanding that there are already a lot of people and organizations out there doing good in all fields and in all walks of life.

I came to the realization that what we needed to do was connect the goodness in order to create a critical mass of people doing good. That way, awareness would be increased and the media, being a powerful force for change, would no longer be able to ignore the massive good in the world.

Good Deeds Day

When I brought the idea to the office about Good Deeds Day, the team at Ruach Tova stepped right up to take the lead and asked to be the organization in charge of the operations of this new annual event.

Each year, Good Deeds Day continues to grow, and it has become an international day. In 2014, more than 580,000 people participated, collectively giving two million hours of volunteer time worldwide. Good Deeds Day has spread to more than fifty countries, where people each do a good deed for the benefit of others or the planet. Cities, companies, and organizations have gone out in masses to volunteer on Good Deeds Day projects, which adds to the camaraderie and bonding within those communities and workplaces. Many workers bring their spouses and children along to help spread the goodness, doing practical hands-on activities that truly make a difference.

Volunteer coordinators are more common now, and your community may well have a volunteer matching service that you can approach if you don't know where to begin. I encourage you to check them out or invite them to your company to make a presentation to your staff. You might just spark some valuable interest, and your employees stand to gain tremendous benefits by making a volunteer match for themselves or for your employees as a group, that they might not have known existed.

So when you hear about Good Deeds Day every year in March, whether it's through TV, radio, social media, or just by word of mouth, join the thousands who are already going out and do a good deed in your own way. What's great about Good Deeds Day is that it's an example of what every day can look like. We have found at Ruach Tova that most people who go out on Good Deeds Day continue volunteering all year-round.

A Workforce That Gives of Itself

Employees at Bank Hapoalim have been personally volunteering in the community since the 1970s, long before Arison Investments took a controlling interest in this huge organization. Yet in the late 1990s, when I started actively promoting social responsibility and giving to the community on a corporate level, they could not imagine what I was talking about because most businesses back then only cared about the bottom line.

But fast-forward to today, we see tremendous change. Bank Hapoalim has been at the forefront of this change in mindset. In practical terms, the Bank has implemented vision and values, step by step, all the way through the organization. Over time, we have seen volunteer commitment levels increase steadily. This is a result of a joint effort of the Bank to engage more and more employees to volunteer and consciously develop new partnerships between the Bank and non-profit organizations.

The focus and efforts have been widening over the years. In 2012, the role of community coordinator was established at each branch, which was a leadership task given to a staff person who wanted to take it on, along with their own regular job. Community coordinators facilitate community activities for their branches and encourage volunteerism. The initiative is highly successful.

In a survey last year, more than one-quarter of the workforce at Bank Hapoalim, some 27%, shared that they volunteer. When the public was surveyed, including bank clients and non-clients, the strongest impression in the minds of the public is that Bank Hapoalim cares about people and social involvement, and that they are partners for life. Today there are dozens of volunteer and community initiatives that have become synonymous with the bank's brand.

While many factors play a part in the bank's success, I do believe that its social responsibility focus has been an important contributor to making Bank Hapoalim number one among the large banks in Israel. It is estimated that the bank touches the lives of more than three million people daily.

Mentorship: Impactful Personal Volunteering

One of the most powerful volunteer opportunities that a person can offer someone else is to become their mentor. For young adults who are establishing their careers, the value of a successful role model in their same field is tremendous. Young professionals today are seeking this kind of connection. I know it can be complex and time consuming given how busy the corporate environment has become; however, if you are the kind of person who wants to make a difference, becoming a mentor might be the right path for you.

There are formal mentoring arrangements, sponsorships of individuals, and organizations that do this kind of thing, but some of the best relationships arise organically, between someone who has something to offer and someone who is seeking that education.

As a business leader, encouraging this unique kind of volunteer relationship in your organization or industry is a forward-thinking action that will pay dividends in the future. Many young students you might mentor now could become valuable employees later on.

I am sure that most of the people who have been gifted with a mentor in their careers will appreciate what they received and will pass it forward in the future.

Although I can't say that I am a mentor in the formal sense of the word, meeting specific people at specific times or giving lectures to students at colleges as some of my colleagues do, I am well aware that I am a mentor, every moment of every day, whether it is to my children, to the employees who work closest to me, or to my vast workforce. Even to the people who approach me through emails, letters, or telephone calls or someone who stops me in the street, I feel the responsibility to be a mentor. I always remember to be a personal example of the kind of world I want to see.

When we speak about being a personal example, what's more important than *Language and Communication?* That's what we explore in our next chapter.

CHAPTER TWELVE

Language &
Communication

LANGUAGE & COMMUNICATION

A range of channels that facilitate the sending and receiving of information, with synchronization, authenticity, respect, and precision, which lead to an understanding of the messages as they are.

Creating a Better World

We learn language and communication from the time we are born. Even before that, it is said that babies know their parents' voices. As we grow up, language and communication touches every part of our daily lives, impacting us directly and deeply.

Even before babies can speak, they learn the sound of words and they feel communication from their parents through touch, emotion, energy, lullabies, and baby talk. And so it is throughout our lives that there are many levels of how we communicate that go far beyond just the spoken word. In our own definition of this value within the *Doing Good Model*, we call these levels "a range of channels that facilitate the sending and receiving of information."

In our daily interactions, we communicate just as much, if not more, through the energetic field that surrounds us when we interact with others; they can feel if we are genuine in what we are saying, and we can sense from them if they are responding in an authentic way to us. We all have emotions that come into play, and patterns of communication that we learned as children. Then there are different cultural and societal norms that affect how we communicate with others. This adds up to a diverse range of channels that we draw on in order to give and receive messages daily.

The model's goal is to ensure that what we are thinking, what we are feeling, and what we are saying are all in alignment. Then we also have to be aware of whether or not the messages we are sending are being received as we intend. With the world becoming more and more transparent, those around you will see the truth as it is. If you are not truly authentic and aligned, your messages can be misread and misunderstood.

I truly believe that if we want to create a better world, we need to start by improving the conversation. The conversation begins with one's discussion with oneself and goes out further into our relationships. Our choice of words reflects our consciousness. If we have a higher consciousness, it will clearly show in our speech and how we approach our lives.

Through mindful communications, we can build bridges and connect with others around us in a positive way.

The Power of the Spoken Word

Words have the power to build people up or tear them down. I don't think enough people are aware of how their words and their style of communication truly affect other people. While you can't control how other people will receive your messages, you can be sensitive and do your best to be authentic and thoughtful in what you say to others. It doesn't matter if you are speaking directly to them or about them while they are not present, the message is still received; people can feel it.

The other skill to practice is listening and becoming aware of the reactions you are getting from those around you. If someone tells you, "It's okay," and yet their vibration is telling you that it's really *not* okay, then this causes confusion and miscommunication. By actively listening to all of their channels, you can tell if your messages are being received as you intended them. In this way, language and communication involves both speaking and listening in equal importance.

So many good things happen when the channels of communication are open and working well, and so much chaos is caused when they are not. I believe that there is not a single person in the world who hasn't had to deal with the results of poor communication at some point in their lives, but then again, if you look back in your life, you have also quite likely had times when you were able to connect deeply with someone else, or you had a really productive meeting, and communication was effortless. Everything clicked.

If you want to have better relationships in all areas of your life, I believe that it all starts with language and communication. When we learn how to communicate so that the outcome is positive, peaceful, and happy, we all win.

This is very evident in our personal relationships, but it is also particularly true in business. Within the workplace, when you have to deal with difficult communications, it is exhausting and depleting. Precious time is lost in dealing with office politics, trying to smooth things over and make peace between people and departments that are simply not communicating effectively. Too often, language is used detrimentally to serve the ego. So many times, you see grown people talking and acting like five-year-olds. These reactions, although natural, can be changed.

To get back to being productive and creative at work, I would encourage bringing people to your team who can speak in a straightforward and truthful manner, while still caring and being professional. These people are aware of how to use language and communication to build, connect, and be productive.

Tunes of Communication

Just as I mentioned before, when I spoke about egos and about five-year-olds, that was the norm in my business as well. Each day, we saw people getting hurt, people blaming others, and their egos rising as they felt they were being backed into a corner. Voices were loud, and occasionally you could hear the shouting in the hallways. And just like many offices, the coffee area was known for gossip. I'm sure everyone can relate.

I know that change always begins within me, within myself, and so that meant that change in business had to start within my *own* business. The situation improved when I focused on having people in my group who had the same vision and lived it. For those who did not, there was a natural parting of ways. I wanted everyone in our group to realize that you can be professional and prosperous while at the same time being caring and respectful to oneself and to others.

The *Doing Good Model* completely transformed our environment. Our organization is now comprised of the kind of people I am proud to say are my partners in creating positive change in everything that we do and everywhere that we conduct business.

I would like to tell you a story that reminded me of how far we have come, how our language and communication, both inward and outward, has completely changed. The story involves a past supplier to our offices who wanted the chance to do business with us once again. He called one of my managers, aggressively requesting that he be allowed to work with us.

This man yelled at my manager, making all kinds of accusations, and demanded that she reinstate his services. His rude and disrespectful language might have been acceptable in the past, but my manager felt the difference in how we speak to one another in the group and how grating his tone of voice was to her. She immediately came to me, knowing that this supplier was someone who I knew from the past, and described to me how she felt. She was distraught and did not know what to do and how to reply to him. We hadn't heard that old kind of tune for so long, the kind that is filled with anger, aggression, and blame, that it sounded foreign to her.

I was so happy and relayed to her that instead of being distraught we should look at it in a positive light, understanding how far we have come. In the past, we would have thought nothing of it. That kind of talk was usual, but today, having an environment that is quiet, peaceful, professional, and respectful, his voice seemed like nails on a chalkboard, screeching. The tune that we have become used to is pleasant, while his tune was disturbing. I told her to go back to the supplier and explain to him that this is not the manner that we wish to communicate in. Our doors are always open for consideration with those who want to do business with us in a respectful, professional, and peaceful manner.

After she and I spoke, I thought, wow, how great that the new tunes in our office environment are filled with camaraderie, enjoyment, creativity, and unity.

Our team simply does not choose to do business in the old way any longer, and this example illustrates how the corporate culture has shifted internally at the Arison Group, to the point where those same standards of proper and respectful communication are required from everyone we deal with, including our external suppliers.

Truly Changing Corporate Culture

My passion was to introduce the thirteen values–based model internally and across the board. In order to do this, we had to find a way to instill the values in practical terms, not just theoretically. The two chairmen of my businesses and of my philanthropic organizations suggested that we introduce a few values at a time through the forums that they created. Me being the kind of person that I am, I continued to voice my wish that the model be integrated completely, all thirteen values. To all of our surprise and delight, after taking part in the first forums, our employees wanted *more*!

A great example happened at Salt of the Earth. The manager took the initiative with regard to the value of Language and Communication, and I was excited and proud to hear about them taking the lead. They didn't wait for us to establish a forum in Language and Communication (which does now exist) because they already knew how important this value was to their operation, and being part of the model, they ran with it.

Here's how it happened. Within Salt of the Earth, the managers chose to introduce this value as a way to deal with the challenge of diversity within their workforce. Many workers at their facilities spend their working days side by side and they have to communicate, but these workers come from such a wide range of different cultures, and they speak different languages—including Hebrew, Arabic, English, Russian, and other European languages.

As soon as the senior management team at Salt of the Earth began to introduce the topic of language and communication, and presented a manager's workshop about these principles, they began to see improvements. It has now filtered from the top to middle management and to the full workforce, with everyone understanding better how the various levels and styles of communication can affect the workplace environment.

It has made a big difference for managers to know how and why messages can go wrong, and they have changed their approach and their practices accordingly. So even though they have a hugely diverse workforce, there is far more respect, tolerance, and understanding in the organization, and less time is needed to smooth over misunderstandings and settle confusion.

As I always talk about the ripple effect, the news from Salt of the Earth quickly spread to the rest of the Group, speeding things up to create an across-the-board Language and Communication forum. Although I have only met with this forum once so far, it's amazing to see the enthusiasm and the great ideas that are coming out of it.

For instance, they are working on what they are calling at the moment a *positive translation dictionary*, with ideas flowing from employees from all our business entities and non-profit organizations on how we can change our language from the negative to the positive. This will include words and phrases. Some of the suggestions are: instead of saying "no problem," we can say "happily." Instead of saying, "I can't" or

"I don't want to," you can say, "I'll check another option" or "perhaps we can try another direction." Instead of saying, "I can't be there at five p.m.," one can say, "I'll be happy to arrive at six." They are even having fun with creating a name for the dictionary. What's so great is that just the conversation around this value has already created change.

The Ripple Effect

We had a young man who worked for us a few years ago as part of our marketing and communications department. He also worked as a project manager with our family foundation. He moved on to another job just before we began implementation of the *Doing Good Model*. However, he was involved in various aspects of communication while we were working as a team on creating the definitions for the values. He has stayed in touch, and it's great to see how he has taken what he learned from the Arison Group and moved it forward in his new job.

He works at one of the most successful media platforms in Israel. I asked him to share with us a story, one that illustrates how the values that he worked on with us are rippling out and reaching completely new audiences.

Here's how he explained it. "About two years ago, we started working on the redesign of the news edition. We were trying different ways to reformat the news, and I started thinking about how to break the boundaries of the current format. I wanted to leave the audience with the idea that not all news is bad news. I knew from my previous job at the Arison Group that many good deeds are done all the time, but positive stories from the general public rarely get reported on newscasts.

"Usually when people listen to the news, it is all about deaths, disasters, and catastrophes. I proposed to the general manager the possibility of making a positive closure to each newscast," he explains. "The manager loved the idea immediately, and all news editors were instructed to look for a 'good news report' to wrap up each news broadcast, as the final item."

The media outlet has always been quite traditional in its news coverage, so this kind of editorial decision was really impressive. It takes a different kind of creativity to find and report on good news items, but the people really embraced this new approach. In this way, the media outlet is training journalists to open their minds to see not only the hard news, but to also see the goodness in society and learn to report on all kinds of stories.

This young man smiled when he thought back on the initiative that he put forward, realizing where the mindset came from. "This example relates to the type of thoughts I was exposed to when I worked at the Arison Group, especially during the internal meetings we had with Shari herself," he remembers. "I think that the messages I was exposed to at the Arison Group were a bit like a 'chip' planted in my head, but in a good way."

Switched At Birth: Communication
Without Saying a Word

There is a TV series that I really like called *Switched at Birth*. It premiered on ABC Family Channel in 2011 and is now in its fourth season. It is a family show that revolves around the lives of two teenage girls who were switched at birth in the hospital by mistake, and who grew up in very different family situations.

When these two girls met at the age of sixteen, they ended up becoming like sisters, sharing two sets of parents, where one family had to suddenly learn American Sign Language (ASL) in order to communicate with their newly discovered biological daughter, who became deaf as a young child. The show presents not only complex family dynamics, but also the impact on friendships, school, and what dating can be like between the hearing and non-hearing.

I found out online that this was the first mainstream TV series to have several recurring actors who are deaf or hard-of-hearing. I enjoyed that some episodes featured a few scenes that were shot using just sign language. In fact, I was quite amazed that one whole episode was done this way, without a spoken word. Instead they relied on sign language, music, facial expressions, and emotions to convey the story for that episode. It truly touched me, and I experienced a world that I am not a part of, in quite an extraordinary way.

I was deeply moved by this episode and this series. It showed how media companies can create such compelling content that is so true to life and fulfilling to watch. I literally went into their lives. To me, the whole series has made a huge impact, illustrating what can be accomplished when a TV station, producers, writers, actors, and a full professional team commit themselves to relaying messages that at times are life changing to the viewers, and doing so in a positive way. In this case, it gave me and thousands of other viewers a look into a world that is unseen for some of us, and it helps us to understand both the strengths and the challenges faced by people who are deaf or hearing-impaired.

The positive impact that we have seen created by some in the field of media can be replicated in any other field one works in. I believe that any family, business, organization, media, community, country, planet, and more (in other words, all circles of life) can be built or destroyed based on our individual and collective language and communication skills. It is my heart's desire to relay this message, hoping that people will put their minds, hearts, and actions into communicating in a way that will build a peaceful and prosperous future for us all. And how fitting it is that our next value is *Sustainability.*

Activate Your Goodness: A Broader Scope of Influence

CHAPTER THIRTEEN

Sustainability

SUSTAINABILITY

Protecting and enhancing existence through economic, social, and environmental balance—for us and for the generations to come.

Defining Sustainability

After many years of talking about sustainability when no one understood what I was talking about, today, not only is the term widely understood, it is defined in many different ways. Sustainability means a various array of things to a wide range of people and organizations. For a long time, anyone I came in contact with thought that my vision and my life's work is sustainability. However, I have said, and continue to say, that although sustainability is an important part of my vision and work, there are in fact many parts to my overall vision, which you have been already hearing about in this book of the *Doing Good Model.*

Our definition of Sustainability that we came to in our collective group is "protecting and enhancing existence through economic, social, and environmental balance—for us and for the generations to come."

Wikipedia defines Sustainability in this way: "Sustainability is the endurance of systems and processes. The organizing principle for sustainability is sustainable development, which includes the four interconnected domains: ecology, economics, politics, and culture."[4]

The Financial Times Lexicon, which is the definitive source for business terms, explains Sustainability this way: "Business sustainability is often defined as managing the triple bottom line—a process by which companies manage their financial, social, and environmental risks, obligations, and opportunities. These three impacts are sometimes referred to as profits, people, and planet."[5]

Sustainability can be many different things to many different people, businesses, and organizations. Each entity focuses sustainability on what suits its own individual vision. For a person, it could be recycling. For a bank, sustainable loans. A transportation company could be focusing on renewable energy. Construction companies might focus on eco-friendly

---

[4] http://en.wikipedia.org/wiki/Sustainability (Date accessed: Dec 31, 2014).
[5] http://lexicon.ft.com/Term?term=business-sustainability (Date accessed: Dec 31, 2014).

materials and replenishing nature. A food company might put their emphasis on animal rights and organic food. So as you can see, there are endless possibilities for sustainability and many different aspects of caring for the triple bottom line: people, planet, and profit.

At this point in our human evolution, a social consciousness is developing, where people realize it is important to look at the long-term effects of our actions. The world is actively seeking sustainable solutions and finding that business is a powerful platform for positive action, as a way to impact people, society, and the planet with equal consideration for all.

Within the Arison Group, the value of Sustainability was first applied at Shikun & Binui since that is the vision of the company. Shikun & Binui is our global infrastructure and real estate company, which constructs sustainable projects worldwide. The company also educates their employees on why this is so critically important, so they know that they are part of something bigger.

Implementing sustainable practices has been transformational, and our companies continue to win prestigious awards and globally recognized certifications. For example, most of our real estate development projects in Israel have been constructed according to leading local and global environmental standards. Some are even designed and built according to the LEED (Leadership in Energy and Environmental Design) Gold Standard, which is a highly respected American rating system for the design, construction, operation, and maintenance of green buildings, homes, and neighborhoods. LEED is an initiative of the U.S. Green Building Council (USGBC).

In 2013 Life and the Environment, the Israeli umbrella organization of environmental NGOs (non-governmental organizations), awarded Shikun & Binui its *Green Oscar*, which is also known as the *Green Globe*, to recognize the company's outstanding achievement in environmental protection in Israel and its green business initiatives. Shikun & Binui was the first company in Israel of its size and magnitude to win that award.

Sustainability in Large-Scale Projects

At Shikun & Binui and at Miya, the focus is always on making sure that our construction, infrastructure, and water projects are done on a fully sustainable basis. Although our intent is constant and our knowledge is broad, these projects are extremely complex. We work in different countries around the world with different cultures, languages, and challenges.

We want all of our projects to be a win-win situation where all parties benefit. This also includes the environment, the people who live in the specific areas, local training and employment, and keeping the projects sustainable for many years to come.

Here are just a few examples of the ways we apply the principles of sustainability and deliver more than what the contract calls for, doing what is best for the environment. Governments and citizens in emerging countries can benefit highly from the knowledge and innovation brought in global companies involved in large scale projects. We consider all of the ramifications that go into building a road, constructing a bridge, or refurbishing a water-delivery system. A wide range of potential impacts are fully researched and considered upfront, before any work is done on such large-scale projects, or projects of any size really. We approach each job from a values-based perspective and look for ways to add value to the local community, while protecting its precious natural resources at the same time.

Most often, we build into the contract the specific natural preservation activities that we know will have to be done to protect the environment during the timeframe of the overall project. Perhaps reservoirs will have to be drained for a period of time and refilled afterward; this can be hugely complex but not impossible. Trees may need to be taken down, and if so, they will be replaced with new trees at the end, or where possible, mature trees are dug up first and moved to a temporary place for a given time, so the company can move them back to their original sites just before the overall project is completed.

At many project sites, the top layer of fertile soil is scraped up, carefully set aside, and then replaced once the construction or restoration work is completed. This fertile soil is hugely important to the community for its future, so every caution is taken to preserve it for future use. Likewise, natural animal habitats and waterways are as carefully preserved as possible. It is not unusual for the construction teams at Shikun & Binui to discover gaping holes in the landscape that might have been caused by large construction projects that were done in the past by other companies, before we entered the picture. If leftover damage to the landscape was not properly dealt with by a previous contractor from years gone by, the company makes a point to properly fill in those holes so that they do not pose any further safety concerns for current or future residents to deal with. Once we leave a project site, we wish it to be in the best possible shape, because we care about the impact on the local community and the natural environment.

An Extraordinary Natural Habitat

Our Salt of the Earth operations are impressive in many ways, but what I love about this company is that the employees understand and respect their close connection to the natural world, and they have truly created a place where animals, nature, and human beings live in harmony while the work of the day is being done.

The company produces salt in a natural and clean process of solar vaporization of onshore pools of sea water. Over the years, the company has created a bird and animal sanctuary around these pools, and each year thousands of aquatic birds naturally migrate to the pools, where they nest and thrive. Salt of the Earth has developed cooperative relationships with the International Bird Watching Center, the Society for the Protection of Nature in Israel, and the Israel and Nature Parks Authority with regard to preserving the habitat not only for birds but also sea turtles and other species.

Schoolchildren and visitors of all ages are encouraged to combine bird watching and other natural activities from newly developed lookout points located around the salt water pools. From these vantage points, you can see a wide variety of birdlife, including ducks, plovers, yellow wagtails, pipits, and terns. As well, you might see a flock of flamingos, which is really incredible, and the acacia trees to the west provide shelter to a variety of songbirds.

Salt of the Earth has taken great care to develop its production processes in a safe and environmentally friendly manner. The company does not use chemicals or toxins in the refinement process, and the ponds are sealed so that underground aquifers are protected. The company has also developed these ponds over what was non-agricultural land, thus changing the land from desert to productive land.

The salt-production process at Salt of the Earth uses wind and sun as the main energy sources to fuel production, thereby reducing the carbon impact on the environment and harnessing clean energy to fuel its activities. All these choices make a positive impact on the environment and regenerate unproductive land in a way that attracts natural animals to a new and productive landscape.

Sustainable Banking

It is interesting to me the many ways that the companies in our group find to apply the principles of Sustainability. A new initiative at Bank Hapoalim takes the idea of Sustainability and applies it to the process of bank lending. One focus in particular is on managing credit problems that customers are experiencing in a more sustainable way.

When customers are overdrawn or behind on their debt payments, the traditional way of dealing with this was for the bank to refer the matter to a collections process and involve legal counsel to force the clients to repay their debt. The bank realized that this is not a particularly sustainable way to do business. Customers don't tend to return to the bank in the future if legal procedures are brought against them in regard to their debt problems.

So Bank Hapoalim set out to find a more sustainable and humane solution, one that was far better in the long run for all concerned. They decided to make a transition from collection-oriented processes to customer recovery and retention. The thought was that taking legal actions or canceling someone's credit cards might collect some of the outstanding debt, but it's really just a Band-Aid approach that doesn't do anything to improve the person's long-term financial situation.

So to begin with, the bank educated managers about this new approach, one where bank employees would appreciate the bank's responsibility to help customers in hardship, and create win-win solutions together, instead of initiating uni-lateral actions, as had been the practice in the past.

Instead of the bank placing a call to a customer demand-ing payment, the bank now contacts customers to explore the reasons for the problem and how they can help. Very often, it is happening because the customer just doesn't understand how to manage their finances or because of something unexpected that the customer experienced, such as a sudden job loss, the transition of leaving a marriage, serious health concerns, accidents, or other hardship.

Solutions for a Sustainable Future

The transition to the new approach has proven to be highly successful. I was told that the customers responded very well when they were given a great range of options, tools, and knowledge. They were offered help in the form of apps for their phones, website resources, budget-management advice, and other education and services, and they are now able to make informed decisions that guide them toward their own financial freedom.

Bank employees are now given more leeway and creative solutions to offer to customers in an effort to truly help them through what might be a very difficult time. For the really tough cases, a dedicated team of professionals was set up to create complex solutions with the customer, devising a wide range of solutions and tools that will work for the customer to help repair their financial issues, and also retain them as a customer in the long term.

Feedback has been very positive about this new initiative. At the branch in Holon, for example, there has been an increase in customer satisfaction with regard to the quality of service and in overall satisfaction with bank services. There has been a decline in discount debt, which is a debt instrument that is issued at a price below its face value. Along with this, the bank's risk level has improved, and there was an increase in credit performance. Fewer customers were transferred to collections, and the branch even noticed that more relatives of those satisfied customers were choosing to bank at Bank Hapoalim.

The Circle of Life

Another one of the really wonderful examples of sustainable practices that I have heard about recently came to me from Ravit Barniv, who used to be chairman of Shikun & Binui of the Arison Group. She is now chairman of the largest food group in Israel. She asked to meet with me to share how she took the sustainable education that she absorbed from our group, and how she was moving it forward to create sustainability within the new company she joined.

She was so excited to share with me how she took that knowledge into a whole other industry, and I was equally excited to hear about it. To me, true success is the impact you have on others and your surroundings. Hearing about how our dedicated work on implementing values in business, including sustainability, has reached far and beyond our group is true validation. How great is that!

The company that Ravit leads now is Tnuva, a company that is virtually in every household in Israel in the form of fresh dairy products and other food items. She described how the various aspects of their operations and supply chains have become even more integrated and sustainable than ever before, forming a circle of life that reaffirms what positive and strategic business practices can accomplish.

Their story starts at a kibbutz dairy farm, which supplies the dairy production plant with all the milk that is used to create their cottage cheese and white cheeses. The factory, which is also owned by the kibbutz, supplies a local dairy production plant with plastic cottage cheese containers, which are now recyclable.

While the dairy products are being made, whey is produced as a natural by-product. The whey is transferred to another local factory where the lactose and proteins are extracted for use and any remaining whey is disposed of through wastewater.

The wastewater then goes to a large water-purifying facility, which was established by the dairy company, where the whey-water mixture is turned into reclaimed water. The reclaimed water is then used for irrigation of cornfields at the original kibbutz. The corn that is grown is sold to Sunfrost, which is the leading frozen vegetable company in Israel and a subsidiary of the dairy company. The leftover cobs of corn become cow feed for the kibbutz's cattle.

She also talked to me about caring for the overall food chain, including how animals are grown. She now understands the importance of the circle of life and that we all have a part to play. With that, she added the fact that she is leading a public company, and therefore things take time and are a process, which of course I completely understand.

There is no doubt in my mind that most of the people who work in my group, or who have moved on to other companies, carry with them values in their minds and hearts and will continue to grow the circles of values-based leadership and sustainable impact. All of those people are bringing *Added Value for Humanity*, the value we will talk about next.

CHAPTER FOURTEEN

Added Value
for Humanity

ADDED VALUE FOR HUMANITY

*The courage and ability to lead to a better world by
connecting between thought, emotion, and actions, and the
fulfillment of the universal potential.*

The Depth of a Value

Consider the depth in these words: "The courage and ability
to lead to a better world by connecting between thought, emotion, and actions, and the fulfillment of the universal potential."

This definition of Added Value for Humanity is of course
the definition that was created collectively, as with all the other
values. This specific value comes from the vision of Arison
Investments. I would, however, like to give my own individual
perspective by breaking down the definition into parts.

Why "courage"? For me, I believe it takes extreme courage to lead a vision that is before its time. No matter how much you explain, people do not get it at first. It takes courage to connect to one's own truth and go against the stream. But what I can tell you is that, in the end, it pays off.

Why "ability"? One has to know what they are capable of achieving. I might want to be an opera singer, but if I don't have a voice, I don't think it's going to be possible. So, therefore, in business—or any endeavor, for that matter—while it takes vision, it also takes ability. Do you have the resources that you need? The right people? The right environment? What is your strong suit?

The connection between thought, emotion, and action is extremely important, in my eyes. Thought is your intention. What is it that you want to accomplish? Emotion is doing from the right place, from the heart, from caring, from the will to make a positive concrete difference.

Action is the manifestation of the intent and the will. Many people have wonderful ideas, a pure heart, and the will to do something that they are passionate about. Action makes it happen, makes it come alive.

I see the fulfillment of the universal potential as potential that is out there on so many different levels. Fulfillment within one's company comes in many ways. One way would be the fact that you care about how the individual employees feel and if they feel personally fulfilled. Fulfillment of the universal potential goes out in ever-widening circles, focusing on always having a win-win situation, whether it is with suppliers, clients, advisors, partners, and so forth. Going out even further, the universal potential can be manifested in ways like environmental sustainability, an abundance of water, spreading inner peace and goodness, and so much more.

This value is defined in such a broad way that it has endless facets to it. It's deep and wide. I just gave you some of my thoughts and examples, but I am sure that each individual or organization can expand on it even further.

Arison Investments

Arison Investments is the investment company that leads and holds a stake in, or fully owns, the business companies that I have already talked about. Efrat Peled is the CEO and chairman of Arison Investments and works with a highly skilled and professional team. The company is active in finance, real estate and infrastructure, renewable energy, and water and salt. Our goal is to create financial returns alongside added value for humanity while preserving the earth's natural resources. We aspire to achieve global, social, economic, and environmental balance and we view universal challenges as opportunities to create business innovations.

Our long-term investment strategy focuses on encouraging large-scale ventures that provide a values-based response to the basic needs of large populations, while balancing between people, profit, and planet. Our choices for investment are directed toward high financial returns, while bringing about a new business reality that is foremost environmentally and socially responsible. The financial results we achieve from this approach coincide equally with the result we see in values implementation, setting a benchmark that we are proud of.

Creating a Portfolio with Responsibility

Let me first differentiate between Arison Investments and my personal investment portfolio. Arison Investments is an operational entity that has a management team, employees, and subsidiary companies. Arison Investments invests with a moral compass, and so do I with my personal assets. But it's even more complicated to invest in that way with large sums of money that are distributed between many different financial institutions and money managers.

I have always looked at my investments from a moral outlook. It has always been important to me, and I have given instructions that I would not invest in guns, tobacco, alcohol, or anything that harmed animals or hurt the environment. This was not an easy task. For many years, money managers complained that it was practically impossible to do what I asked. In the past, in all of my investment documents, my wishes were noted, but could not be promised.

It's amazing to see that, with my leadership and the leadership of my team at my family office, change has been created over time. We actually educated financial institutions that

I have been investing with in a different way of looking at investing.

With this in mind, the family office worked together with the financial institutions to create precise standards that money managers could use. My team then could come back to me with suggestions for investments that are aligned with my wishes. It's important to note that with any vision or change, building a strategy and implementing it takes time, and the same goes for my personal portfolio. Although I have already seen incredible change, that change is continuing to evolve within my portfolio and with everyone I work with.

The investment strategy that we put into place focuses on companies that have strong cash flow positions, good dividends, and reasonable risk, and that represent a balance of sectors overall. I like to see that companies I invest in are sustainable in their practices and publicly traded. We look to see if a company has been recognized by global indexes or other credible third-party sources that screen for true adherence to positive quality measures, such as corporate social responsibility or sustainable manufacturing practices.

Fortunately, there are many companies in the world that provide basic needs and services to people in sustainable ways using sustainable energy sources, efficiently and humanely, and these are my preference. Some of the companies we invest in are not quite there yet, but we can see their process and concrete actions for positive change. This is important to me. I feel that this investment approach adds another facet to the value of Added Value for Humanity.

Collaboration for Change

Another way that we do our part in fulfilling the universal potential and adding value for humanity is through our work in philanthropy. For more than twenty years, The Ted Arison Family Foundation has been our group's philanthropic arm in Israel. My eldest son, Jason Arison, is the chairman of the foundation and Shlomit de Vries is the CEO.

The family foundation makes impactful social investments through strategic philanthropy. Social investments are in the fields of health, education, disabilities, populations in distress, and the arts. These are in addition to our unique vision ventures that include Volunteering, Inner Peace, and the various *Doing Good* platforms.

Here is just one example of how the foundation contributes in many ways to giving added value for humanity. One area of social investment that the foundation has been keenly interested in over the years is helping to fund NGOs that serve people with disabilities.

About three years ago, along with other foundations and corporate interests, Shlomit (representing the family foundation) joined and helped form a round table to benefit people with disabilities. The focus is on helping a wide range of people who have various challenges, such as cognitive impairment, physical issues, autism, blindness, hearing impairment, or mental disabilities; challenged populations; and those with other issues.

It was felt that a coordinated effort from the primary funders in this field, both non-profit and corporate, could be beneficial, in addition to each group still giving from their own resources in their own ways as they had done before. The government also funds services and needs with regard to people with disabilities, and this round table was not set up to replace or hinder that essential support either.

Instead, the round table chose as their first major focus to create a *Positive Approach Index for Accessibility*, which was completed and published in 2013. They felt this was hugely valuable because it used details gathered from research and surveys to put into one document a standard approach for how persons with disabilities should be able to access essential services in their communities, and how this can be improved.

The collaborative efforts of the round table are as much about raising awareness and improving attitudes as about accessibility, but each element is essential in the bigger picture. The key message for government, society, and employers is that this population is part of us, and we need to treat them as such and help them bring out their highest human potential, the same way we would with any person.

The Simplicity of Added Value

When we think about how we can add value for humanity, I am reminded of the many ways that our infrastructure company, Shikun & Binui, and our water efficiency company, Miya, approach their work on large-scale projects around the world.

Whenever they enter another country, before they begin the project work, they make a point to meet with the local leaders of the community so they can understand the culture and the needs of the people who live there. Our teams approach this from a values-based perspective, wishing to set up in advance as positive a relationship as possible, a bond that will be a lasting connection between the company and the community.

By establishing these relationships early, the company can see what other needs might be in the community and think about how the company can help the residents to adjust to the changes that are coming as part of the big construction or water project that is being undertaken.

An example would be where they might be constructing a modern highway through a community that only had a very narrow road before. Children and adults might not understand the dangers of crossing a large roadway, so the company would give them lessons in basic road safety, how to walk along the road, and how to cross in the right way.

With regard to water projects in a developing country, small rural communities can suddenly have running water for the first time. The company has been active in teaching people basic hygiene methods, such as hand washing, and explaining water conservation techniques that this population just never had any idea about before this point. It was just not a part of their society.

Workplace development is another factor that our companies take the lead on. Employing local workers sometimes involves training them in the most basic workplace safety rules, such as how to use protective clothing on the worksite, how to handle tools, how to avoid getting hurt while working, and how to communicate effectively while at work as part of a team.

As these workers pick up new skills by being part of the overall team, they gain valuable employment skills for the future. In a similar way, local engineers and technicians gain new experience that they can add to their resume by being part of a large and complex infrastructure project that is local to them in their own country.

Instead of bringing in large workforces from abroad, training these workers and engineers locally in itself adds value. By providing education and skills, we are bringing added value to the individual. When those individuals continue with their expertise, long and far after we have completed our projects, they are then able to keep the project they worked on sustainable over time. This then brings additional added value to that region.

Other times, our people find unique ways to improve the lives of those we meet when in the field. One example was when the team from Miya realized that a local primary school did not have water because it had no working taps. The workers from Miya took some of their free time and accessed materials donated through the company to replace the faucets and lavatories at the school. They also taught the children about water, how to treat it with respect, and how washing their hands properly would help keep them healthier.

The feedback that we received was that the children went home taking what they learned to their parents, grandparents, and siblings. The children also completed an art project on their new knowledge about water and were thrilled to show it to the team at Miya.

Singing for a Cause

One aspect of our process at the Arison Group around the values and the *Doing Good Model* was a workshop that was delivered by a group of professors we are working closely with from different universities. Through the research, the workshop included a wide range of examples of value implementation from organizations around the world. This included university case studies, documentary-style videos, and other thought-provoking articles that had been published or posted on the Internet.

When we discussed the value of Added Value for Humanity, one of the articles they shared with us was about the phenomenon of gathering public support for a cause by rallying thousands of people. In the traditional sense, rallies are a form of a march, to build awareness and create change. When I think about rallies, my heart's desire is that they always be peaceful and that the messages be focused on solutions and unity.

The impact of large gatherings was hugely increased when popular music celebrities entered the mix, and media coverage went worldwide. Suddenly, the cause, whatever that might be, sometimes became its own spectacle and numbers of participants jumped from thousands, to tens of thousands, to millions of people coming together for a cause.

One of the earliest of this style was the Concert for Bangladesh in 1971. People were suffering greatly from starvation and loss of lives due to the raging war in the area, compounded by natural disasters. They desperately needed aid from the world, but their pleas remained largely unheard until a huge public concert was held in New York City involving George Harrison, Bob Dylan, Ringo Starr, Eric Clapton, and a few other high-profile musicians.

The concert raised more than $250,000 for UNICEF that went toward the humanitarian cause in Bangladesh. This was a huge benefit to what was before a little-known cause in the West. The event showed for one of the first times, in a big way, the power of music and fame to influence people toward social change.

On July 13, 1985, an astounding 1.4 billion people were impacted, feeling in their hearts and minds *one single cause*, as they were riveted to TVs and radios for the original Live Aid. The concert was led by the rock band Queen, joined by others, and the spectacle was produced by Bob Geldof. The cause that united one-fifth of all people on our earth that day was the Ethiopian famine crisis. Before the event was over, it had raised more than $200 million for famine relief.

So as you can see, it takes one person with a passion to ignite a worldwide movement, and a song in one's heart has the capacity to reach the universe. *We Are All One.*

CHAPTER FIFTEEN

We Are All One

WE ARE ALL ONE

Each person has his or her uniqueness.
All of us comprise the whole and constitute part of it.

The Many Faces of Humanity

We are all one. Each person in the world has his or her own individuality. As I see it, it's similar to the fact that we each have fingerprints, and no fingerprint is like another. The same goes for our individual signal. What I mean by signal is the tone, the vibration that we resonate from ourselves outward to the world.

Although we are all souls and all human beings, and it might seem on the surface that we are the same, we each have our own uniqueness. With that in mind, we are all part of the whole. The whole picture. One could be a part of a family, a part of a community, or a part of a country, and all of humanity is a part of our planet. Our planet is a part of the universe.

Therefore, no matter how you look at it, we are all one. We are all a part of a bigger picture and we all have a part to play. Whether the part we are playing is with a conscious mindset or not, we each need to take responsibility for our collective future.

Some people think that if something is happening that is detrimental to our collective future, but is not close to their home or close to their heart, it does not affect them. In my opinion, this is an illusion that many of us live with, but the fact is the future of our planet, the future of humanity is in all of our hands. If we want to see a positive future, we need to understand that we are all one and choose to take responsibility for the part that we play.

Creating a Positive Future: Goodnet.org

Individuals and cultures that used to be worlds apart, who for generations would never see or get to know one another, are miraculously only a click away from one another when they discover one another online. The Internet has shown immense power to connect all of us, immediately and personally, one to another.

As a part of what we are doing as a group, both in business and philanthropy, we decided to use the power of the Internet to create a place that highlights all of the good. We developed an interactive digital platform, open to everyone in the world, called Goodnet.org. It is a central meeting place online to share ideas, receive inspiration, and connect with other people worldwide who are also *doing good* in all fields and in all walks of life.

While talking, contemplating, sharing, and finding new ways to *do good*, I believe we can elevate ourselves and our communities to the understanding that we are all one. If we want to see a future that is pure, honest, peaceful, with growth and prosperity, we each need to take individual responsibility for our collective future.

Goodnet has been extremely successful, reaching more than seventeen million people within approximately two and a half years, with one million people joining in every month. It is exciting to me to see the list of countries that in today's world would be defined as enemies, coming together around good. Goodnet also takes part in Good Deeds Day every year in March, and people around the world are able to connect to a cause or a volunteer organization, or make a simple pledge to do good.

I believe that in order to have true transformation, we need a critical mass of people coming together for the benefit of us all. Given that people have their own uniqueness, their own way of seeing things, perspectives, and gifts to give, we can leverage all this potential by bringing people together who put the light on unity with a will to solve problems so that all of us can live in a better world. At the Arison Group, we are doing our part, and we know there are so many others doing their part, so Goodnet's focus is to bring together all those who are doing good to create a critical mass.

Face-to-Face Forums

It has always been my intention and desire that the values within the *Doing Good Model* would filter out beyond our group, and that is already happening in a number of ways. Academics are working with the model and helping to find ways to bring these values alive to university and college students. We are actively developing an online resource that we will launch first internally among our vast workforce, with the idea that it will eventually be made available to the public.

When we began to have meetings internally to find ways to implement the values that make up the *Doing Good Model*, management called these group meetings forums. Anyone who wanted to be part of a forum could join in, understanding that it is above and beyond their regular job. As word spread throughout the group, interest and enthusiasm kept growing, and so did the number of people in each forum.

While I am not a member of the forums, I do get regular updates and I attend the semi-annual forum get-together where all the forums present what has been implemented in all business companies and philanthropic organizations across the group.

After a few years of ongoing successful forums, I was told that so many people wanted to take part in the process that it was hard to continue to have productive meetings. The forums were split into smaller groups, and more forums were created for additional values. Management created a committee that would oversee all forums, and again, employees were invited to be on that committee as well.

The "All One" Connection

The forums changed and grew as a natural evolution. It has been amazing and thrilling to me after so many years of talking, explaining, wishing for change, to see how, now, so many people are on board, so many people connected and doing their part to create positive change. This is happening both within their individual companies or organizations and outwardly to suppliers, clients, communities, and countries that we work in. For me, it is a dream come true.

The next evolution that I have been dreaming of for a really long time is to take what we have created internally within the Arison Group and form a forum for All One that reaches out to other individuals, businesses, and philanthropic organizations.

For a while now, people from outside our group have been approaching us because they have heard that we have a values-based business model and have heard of its success. I have been thrilled to hear from different people of all ages and backgrounds, including social workers, businesspeople, youth workers, government agencies, and others, who want to learn more about the *Doing Good Model* and how they can implement values like these in their own organizations. Some have even taken interest in how they could be part of what we are doing.

Just as we connected people from around the world on Goodnet.org, I believe we can connect people to our *Doing Good Model* and teach them to implement these values, each one in their own environment. As we are an extremely diverse group working in many different fields of business, different types of philanthropic organizations, and in many different countries with diverse people and languages, I believe we have the knowledge and skills to show people outside our group the way to make true, authentic, and positive change.

What's amazing is that we have already created All One in the Arison Group. It sounds simple, but this has taken years. For many years, I asked the different companies to share with the rest of the group what it is that they are doing. It's funny to think that a few years ago, Bank employees didn't know that Arison owned Shikun & Binui. No one knew that Salt of the Earth was connected to us at all or that we had founded a water company called Miya. Employees at the family foundation didn't know that our business companies donate to the community as well. In other words, the left hand didn't know the right, and the right didn't know the left.

Growing "All One"

Each part of the group was totally separate and unaware of the other parts. No matter what I tried to do, for years this did not change. Only after creating the forums did the reality change. People were surprised, impressed, and inspired. The more people who connected, the more values that were being implemented, the more we became All One.

What I really wanted was to take that All One connection that we have created within our group and grow the circles outward to others outside our group. I wanted to create an

All One forum, just like the other forums. However, after many discussions with my management team, we came to the conclusion that this would not be feasible. Having meetings in person with different people from different companies around the world, would not, we believe, have the same kind of impact.

Our will as a group is not just to talk about values, but to find productive and practical ways for implementation. As we grow and reach out to others, we wanted to find a way that we could give the knowledge and the tools to any individual or entity, whether it is a business, big or small, a non-profit organization of any size, a university, or anyone who wants to create change by bringing high, elevated values and transforming them into practical practices.

A Forum for Everyone

That's when we decided that the online platform that we are building for the thirteen-values *Doing Good Model* would be used for the All One forum, rather than creating face-to-face meetings for that particular forum. Working on this process, an online forum has been created. As usual, we have put together a team with representatives from all of our companies and organizations, high-tech experts, and of course, our strategic partners at George Mason University.

I believe that once the process is concluded, we will first use the online tool to connect all of our employees, approximately 30,000 around the world, then offer this tool to universities and university students, and eventually to everyone: individuals, corporations, and organizations. It is funny to say "when the process will be concluded," because nothing is ever concluded in my mind; we are in constant evolution, change, and growth, and one of the features of the online resource is to be able to be flexible and open to change.

As I have described earlier, the forum process provides room for engagement and creativity, and for different people to put forward their own ideas of how a given value can be implemented.

It is exciting to me because I know that same process of implementation can be applied in outside organizations in the same ways we have applied them internally within our group. Just reading about any theory, or hearing about it in a lecture, will not bring it to life. But when a group of people commits to taking tangible action to live from the values they hear about, the *Doing Good Model* is advanced beyond just the words of its definition on the page. The values themselves become a living, breathing, working part of the organization or group, and I would like nothing more than to see values living and breathing everywhere in the world where people gather, whether it is face-to-face or online.

Being "All One" in Business

I would like to share an All One perspective put into practical terms. A formal policy of diversity and inclusion was implemented at Bank Hapoalim. Management and employees agreed that this was the right thing to do, and also good for business. I have heard very positive feedback. What's impressive to me is that it did not come from a mandated quota perspective, but from the heart.

The bank's policy on diversity and inclusion reflects the true fabric of our society, where barriers between cultures come down. People of all faiths, languages, and backgrounds are respected equally in all interactions, as it should be. Whether it is internal, through the hiring process and training, or external, through our services—all the activities of the bank are done with acceptance and understanding of each individual's belief systems and culture.

This may sound simple, but it is extremely complicated. However, doing so has made a profound difference, not only morally, but it has also made every citizen anywhere in the country a potential Bank Hapoalim customer.

As a result, customized products and solutions have now been developed at the bank specifically to meet the needs of people within various sectors. So everything the bank offers, including teaching materials that guide people toward financial freedom, for example, are available and fully relevant to everyone. This includes the many sectors of our society, including the Jewish ultra-religious community, the many different Arab communities, Christians, people who live on kibbutzes (communal living), and immigrants from Russia, Europe, Africa, and more.

In other words, all people in our society have equal access to services, including lessons in financial freedom, customized to their needs and beliefs, to help them to grow and prosper. Likewise, the human resources department treats all individuals equally and customizes their training and scheduling so it is aligned with their language, culture, and beliefs, whatever those might be.

This outlook and practice reflect my belief that although we each have our own individuality, our own uniqueness, we are all one. All of us comprise the whole and constitute part of it. By being all one, and living by it, I believe *abundance* will reveal itself. That's what our next chapter is about.

CHAPTER SIXTEEN

Abundance

ABUNDANCE

Recognizing that everything exists, and responsible action for ensuring "what is."

The Process

I'd like to share with you the process we went through to reach an overall consensus on the values, especially the value of Abundance, even before I explain the value itself. This is important to me because I believe that the process itself shows that when we come together as people, that in itself is creating abundance.

Coming up with the definition for this value, *abundance*, was a long and complex process. I think it was challenging to define because it is very hard for people to accept that everything that we need and want is available to us all. I, for one, believe that abundance is infinite and wanted this as part of the definition, but this was a very difficult concept for others to agree upon.

Although I was passionate about how I personally viewed the definition, for me it was more important that there be a consensus on every word of every sentence to every value. I knew that although the world we live and work in is based on hierarchy and individuality, that will soon change.

I felt in my heart that we as a human race were going toward a world where we are all one, and each individual has an important part to play. I knew that the future would be based on teamwork and togetherness. Therefore, it was important to me to lead by example and create that change already within my group. I did this by making a point that each of the many participants around the table had their voices heard. Although each person had a different perspective and belief system, I knew that in the end, we would create this model together. It would be a win-win situation where everyone would be heard and everyone would be included. Sounds simple, right? Well, it wasn't. But we did it anyway.

It is obvious that when society is fractured, everyone pulling in different directions, the result is not a good one. We saw this happen in the beginning when our group started the process. This is why I felt that it was crucial that I lead the group in a conversation that was authentic and productive.

As I see it, everyone has a place in the larger picture. I see the evolution of our world as people coming together, being heard, contributing their part, and creating positive change. The same goes for any group of people, whether it is at home in a family or within a business environment. When we are trying to create positive change, to create what we want to see happen, we each need to play our part.

When we come together as people, authentic and positive, that is a powerful force. That powerful energy in itself creates abundance.

Abundance for All

In the end, as with all of the other definitions, we came to a unanimous agreement on the definition of Abundance as we collectively saw it. The definition states that abundance is recognizing that everything exists, and responsible action for ensuring "what is."

As I see it, abundance, first and foremost, is a consciousness, a mindset. In order to live an abundant life, you need to believe that it can be so. Let me explain. Abundance can be in just about everything. Many people think of abundance in monetary terms, but abundance, which is the opposite of scarcity, is in all terms, meaning our resources, education, information, relationships, love, and so on.

To live an abundant life, one needs to understand that everything we need already exists. Once we realize this, we need to take responsibility for *what is*, for what exists. An example would be to be conscious of our spending. Many people buy things whether it is food, clothing, or any other products, as if there is no tomorrow. But all those things take resources to produce, whether it is energy, water, animals, and so much more. Are we conscious about that as a collective?

In our personal lives and business lives, all decisions we make impact ourselves and our world in some way, and it is important to make the right decisions for the long term, for the good of all. I see a world where everyone has what they need, and it doesn't have to be at someone else's expense. It's also important to understand that wishes and needs are different for each individual.

A Change of Mindset

As all of the values in the *Doing Good Model* came from the main vision of each company or foundation, so did abundance. Abundance is the vision of Miya. Miya is a water efficiency company that I founded through Arison Investments.

After building the vision, which is to ensure an abundance of fresh water, we set out to learn about the water industry, investing in knowledge and engineering expertise worldwide. We understood, in alignment with our vision, that in order to bring an abundant amount of water to the world, that it already exists and our part is to ensure *what is.*

We entered a field that was known as "water loss" until our company, Miya, came into the industry and changed the term. I was extremely stubborn about changing the name of this field to "water efficiency," as I felt that water loss came from a scarcity mindset, while water efficiency comes from an abundant mindset. The idea of water efficiency is to go into a city or country, learn about its water infrastructure, and determine what is being wasted by leaking underground.

Most people would be extremely surprised to hear that good drinking water, paid-for water, is being lost underground by leaking pipes in cities around the world. Some cities lose anywhere from 30% to 70% of *what is*. The most sustainable and cost-effective way to prevent such losses is to improve the efficiency of our urban water distribution systems. Miya was established to ensure the abundance of fresh water through efficient management of our existing resources. So as you see, there is an abundant amount of water in the world, and by taking responsibility of our water resources and managing them efficiently, Miya can ensure that abundance.

This is amazing proof of manifestation of abundance from our *Doing Good Model*. This is how you take an elated value, a value based on higher consciousness, and bring it down to the business world in practical terms, in practical action. I believe this can be done in any field. It just takes intention, caring, and implementation.

Miya: Abundance in Business

Water is a resource that is essential to all human beings. While it is a natural resource, many parts of the world don't have access to fresh, clean drinking water. Others don't treat the water they have with the understanding of how precious water is. A lot of the water systems around the world are inadequate or crumbling. Our water company, Miya, is dedicated to working closely with municipalities and governments to solve these problems through improving the efficiency of the water infrastructure.

A project in Manila in the Philippines gives an example of what can be done in this industry. When Miya was first engaged, about three million people lacked a connection to the municipal water system, and millions suffered from intermittent supply or very low pressure.

There was more than enough water available, but the water utility in Manila had inherited an aging and highly inefficient water network from the Philippine government, and there were leaks in 65% of its distribution line. The lost water is referred to as non-revenue water (NRW), water that exists in the distribution system but is "lost" before it reaches the customer.

In general, in all of Miya's projects, the company brings comprehensive solutions using low-tech and high-tech knowledge and engineering. In this case, Miya made the reduction of NRW its main priority, and the company suggested a holistic solution that would provide greater water efficiency along with much higher operational levels. Once the pipes were properly fixed and leaks minimized, an incentive-based usage model was also implemented, which led to a significant increase in the level of service.

To build capacity at the ground level and make sure the solution was sustainable, Miya conducted an NRW Management Training certification program that transferred the necessary technical expertise from Miya to employees in Manila, thus ensuring that a local workforce there would have long-term involvement in the newly developed NRW solutions. As a further strategic move, it was suggested that the money saved from the water efficiencies be put into upgrading internal procedures and methodologies.

Overall, the massive project saves 768 million liters of water per day (200 million gallons) allowing 2.6 million additional people to connect to the system on a 24/7 basis. Water pressure and water reliability have both increased and furthermore, the utility has since tripled its yearly income, when compared to its 2008 income level.

Miya is conducting other similar projects in other locations around the world. My son David Arison is vice-president, Global Business Relations for Miya. So as you can see, from a vision that stemmed from a deeply spiritual place, we are able to transform the value of Abundance into practical terms.

Abundance in the Blink of an Eye

Just think about photography and how far we have come over the years. In today's world, we have an abundance of pictures. For most of my life, the way we took photographs was so different than today. We used cameras that needed film, and we worried about how many pictures to take considering that in a roll of film, there were only 12, 24, or 36 pictures available. Film and processing was expensive, so you didn't want to waste the film.

You had to be very selective, and how disappointing it was when you received your pictures back from processing and the images were fuzzy or didn't come out at all. The moment was gone. It was even more heartbreaking when you took pictures of a very special event like a wedding, a birthday party, or a family gathering, and there were no memories to look at if the pictures did not turn out.

Now here we are, not so many years later, and look at the incredible abundance we have with the images we can take. When you want to catch the moment, technology allows you to snap an infinite number of pictures according to your heart's desire. Whether you are using a camera or your phone, endless images are at your fingertips and you can see them immediately. Images are unlimited, they are abundant, so you can capture anything you want, whenever you want.

An Abundance of Information

Not long ago in our collective memory, information was also hard to come by. If you wanted to check facts, look up dates, or find a technical solution to something, you had to refer to a physical book, like a dictionary or encyclopedia. The minute those resources were published, they were out of date, but that was all that people had access to for hundreds of years.

On the flip side, today we have an abundant amount of information at our fingertips through the Internet, available in an instant. All of that information was always out there, in the minds of individuals, but we did not have a physical way to tap into the vast wealth of knowledge and expertise. Today, virtually any issue, challenge, or question that we face can be researched quickly and easily, providing an array of information and endless solutions.

This incredible abundance gives a large number of people access to any information they need. Who would have envisioned that 100 years ago? In my mind, that proves that anything is possible.

Today, although the Internet is bringing us an abundant amount of information worldwide, connecting all of us and giving every human being a voice, it is our choice how we use that information and that voice. Going back to the *Doing Good Model*, let's focus, all of us, on good. Let's raise our voice, positively. We can, as a collective, grow an abundant amount of goodness in the world.

Abundance Consciousness

Let me remind you that I believe that first and foremost, abundance is a consciousness. It is important to understand that the more we focus individually and collectively on scarcity, which is the lack of something, then scarcity is what we will see. Putting the focus on abundance will bring us abundance.

Although it is a consciousness, it is important to understand that in order to create change within ourselves, or within a group, whether it is business or society at large, we need to understand that everything is a process. Set your goal, know that you want to live in abundance, and then take the steps needed to achieve it.

It's important to recognize the small steps, the little achievements. In order to reach the bigger picture, we need to be grateful and recognize what has already been accomplished. Have we changed our mindset? Our thoughts? What's in our heart? It is important to see, really see, our individual and collective actions. Do they reflect the goal we have set forth? I believe that everyone wants to live in abundance.

Understanding this concept, I was extremely upset to see an advertising campaign based totally on scarcity and fear. I believe the intention was a good one: to motivate people toward saving water. But instead of putting the light on the positive, on finding solutions, the campaign was terrifying.

The television advertisement showed a person's face drying up and cracking, to the point of disintegrating into dust. I remember that the key message was "There is no water, we are drying up, there is no water, we are drying up."

This ad was played over and over again. I even remember sharing with some of my employees how I felt about it. I told them that it's amazing to me how people don't see that it is a possibility that tomorrow it could rain, nonstop, and bring us all the water we need. The funny thing was that a short time after sharing my thoughts, it started pouring rain, which lasted several days. It made me smile. I did not see that campaign after that.

As you see, abundance is a mindset. You have to believe, you have to know the possibilities are out there. We can create it. We can create it together.

On that note, let me make a suggestion. Let's create an abundant amount of caring. An abundant amount of compassion. The world needs healing, the world needs love. Let's put our focus, our minds, our hearts, and our actions on creating that love, an infinite amount of love.

Let's create it just because we can.

Platforms for Creating a Better World

CHAPTER SEVENTEEN

From Skeptics to Partners for Change

People Joining In

It has always been my passion to transform things for the better. This has taken place in all parts of my life, whether personal or in business or philanthropy. This, of course, is extremely complicated when talking about a large public company with a board of directors, management team, and thousands of employees. Although it is complicated and takes time, it is that much more rewarding when you see the transformation happening, one more person at a time.

Let me tell you a story about one of my directors, Nehama Ronen. Years ago, when I bought the salt company, it was a public company. In order to make the necessary changes, we at the Arison Group felt that the best way would be to make an offering to buy the company from the public. When this was accomplished, the board of directors of Salt of the Earth was dispersed.

It was suggested to me that I meet with one of the outgoing directors, as I was told that she was extremely impressive and I might want to offer her a seat on the board of directors at Bank Hapoalim. That's when I first met Nehama.

I was impressed by her expertise. She had a long and distinguished career, and she was highly respected by her peers. She had also served in the past as a member of parliament as the Director General of the Ministry of Environment. She is now chairman of the board of ELA Recycling Corporation, a private (non-profit) organization that oversees a large operation for recycling of bottles and beverage containers in Israel. During the meeting with her, I asked her to consider taking a position on the board of Bank Hapoalim, which she did.

She says she recalls our first meeting too, which was about eight years ago, and she remembers so clearly me talking about the values even then, taking a small handwritten list out of my drawer, and speaking from my heart and with such passion about my overall vision. She wasn't at all sure what I was going on about at the time, and she admits that she thought, "Surely this woman is not so naïve as to think that this view of hers, these values, can really change the world?"

But Nehama decided to take a chance and join the board of the bank anyway, feeling that there might be more to these ideas. She was intrigued to find out more. She attended workshops and the early training sessions about the values and about the *Doing Good Model*, watching it evolve along with the rest of us and participating in the process. Nehama remembers the management at the bank also being very skeptical in the beginning, but she has seen the remarkable transformation that has taken place over time.

Positive Change Resonates

"You could see, month to month, how they began gradually to believe," Nehama says with a smile. "Now you can step into any branch and speak to any branch manager and they will be using the same language; you can hear more than 10,000 people across the Bank singing the same song. They believe it and they live it every day."

It was not long before she began to feel the same effects that everyone else was feeling, when she originally began to attend the workshops at the Arison Group. "I got a lot out of this training," she explains. "I learned to put aside my cynicism. I became serious about the values and I paid attention to the tools they gave us in the seminars. I was already a skilled negotiator, but the values training gave me even more tools to use, pure business skills that I didn't expect to gain, but now I use them all the time."

In addition to serving on the board of the bank and heading up the board of ELA, Nehama is also the chairman of the largest logistics company in aviation activities, a company with 2,500 employees.

Taking It Further

Over time, what Nehama discovered by being part of the Arison Group was that once you are part of a group that is always talking about values, you start to absorb it. She was personally affected and thought about Good Deeds Day, how her companies could get involved. Since the employees at the logistics company mostly live near the airport in two smaller cities nearby, she thought that those small cities might be a good place to go to for Good Deeds Day. The overall economy in those places was not very good, and she thought maybe they could use some help.

Nehama asked the employees about it, what could be done. "We thought we would try to go out to the high school, get involved in the communities there, with the older people too, for Good Deeds Day," Nehama told me. "Then the employees said they wanted to continue reaching out and helping. They ended up going out to the high school twice a month, giving lectures, talking about their skills, the aviation industry, and technology. We could see that it opened up the eyes of the students to a future they might also consider."

The next step in the evolution of taking the values out to her other companies was also a natural one for Nehama. "I took some of the values that the Arison Group was using and began to implement them in my other companies, especially Financial Freedom, and I started with the original tools from the seminar," she recalls. Her employees could see the benefits immediately, just as they had within our internal training at Bank Hapoalim.

She went on to talk about the banking industry. "When Shari introduced the idea of financial freedom, over time it became very important at Bank Hapoalim, and it was a big part of the transformation the bank underwent," says Nehama in summary. "Then we started noticing the other banks talking in these same terms, using the same language, and even the government began investing in financial freedom education in the schools."

Her closing comment was that she views the model in comparison to a box of chocolates. You might not be able to eat the whole box of chocolates at one time, but you could eat three or four at a time. Just like the *Doing Good Model*, it would be impossible to truly digest thirteen values all at once, but like the chocolates, you can start with a few today, and tomorrow, you can eat one more.

Profitability: People, Planet, Profit

As the previous story illustrated, I am constantly hearing about how the values in our model are spreading and impacting change. Here are a couple of examples from within our group of the impact the model has on the bottom line. To me, the bottom line not only includes profits, but equally important is the positive impact on people and our planet.

Salt of the Earth was acquired by Arison Investments in 2007. Upon this acquisition, Salt established its mission as "a deep-rooted and ever-renewing company that develops industry that is beneficial to mankind, to the community, and to the environment and that contributes to an ongoing yield to its owners and employees."

The company's commitment to its business, the environment, and the community has been fully informed by implementation of the values within the *Doing Good Model*. Along with the other Arison Group companies and organizations, Salt of the Earth has fully implemented the first four of the values as they were rolled out across the Arison Group in recent years, namely Sustainability, Volunteering, Giving, and Financial Freedom, and they continue to add other values from the model for implementation.

In doing so, Salt of the Earth not only saw an improvement in its reputation in the community, but it also saw impressive increases in production and revenue. Salt of the Earth has been a viable company for more than ninety years. The management did not expect that the new style of values-driven leadership focus would have such an impact, but the results speak for themselves.

Since the acquisition, Salt of the Earth has significantly increased its production efficiency and its sales both domestically and internationally. Over that seven-year period, the company increased its overall income by 40%, and its growth in market share in the salt-shakers sector also increased by 35% (from 12% to 16%). Salt of the Earth attributes its success to the difference that values implementation has had on its employees and on its highly sustainable operations.

Similar and Yet Unique

The original companies that now make up the Shikun & Binui Group have been active since the 1920s, and over the years, those companies had become major players in the fields of construction, real estate, and infrastructure. Prior to 2006, Arison Investments held an interest in this group of companies but was not a controlling shareholder. I saw tremendous potential in this company and admired the depth and experience of its global endeavors, but at the time, the original group of companies was facing instability due to very low levels of equity.

So in 2006, Arison Investments purchased the majority of the employees' shares and took a controlling interest, with a vision to lead the companies through a process of self-renewal and growth. Since then, Shikun & Binui adopted the vision of sustainability and has undergone an extensive process of transformation.

The implementation of the values within the *Doing Good Model* has been a major contributing factor in the dramatic turnaround, along with the fact that Shikun & Binui has built a strong board and management team, ensuring that the right people are now in place. The company has also adopted other business strategies that have aligned this group of companies with the overall vision of Arison Investments that *Doing Good is Good Business.*

Bridges to Prosperity

There are so many huge infrastructure projects that Shikun & Binui is involved with worldwide that I could share with you. The growing list of projects and the positive impacts continues to amaze me. I would like to talk about just one as an example, so you can see how the work of our companies is contributing so much added value for humanity.

The Loko-Oweto Bridge over the River Benue in Nigeria, scheduled to be completed at the end of 2015, will have a dramatic influence on the local society. It is really a series of two bridges that will link the north and the south of the country, and also link the periphery, which are rural areas, with the center of business and commerce. Without this connection, those living in rural areas have only very limited opportunities for advancement, but the bridges will allow them far greater access to jobs, education, health care, and more.

It has been reported by the Nigerian media that with the new access, travel throughout the country will be greatly improved. They also said that the bridge project and the improvements to the series of roads leading up to it will help improve the turnaround of businesses involved in the transportation of goods and services, which will in turn add to the country's GDP. People in the host communities have welcomed the bridge project because they know it will open up their communities to development and growth that was not possible before.

As a global leader in building local and international sustainable living environments, Shikun & Binui is creating various major projects in countries around the world that give added value for humanity. As proof that *Doing Good is Good Business*, the numbers speak for themselves. The compound annual growth rate (CAGR) for equity at Shikun & Binui has increased by 39% from 2007 to the first quarter of 2014. The CAGR for equity and dividend has increased by 53% over that same period of time, ensuring not only stability but sharing of this profitability with all its shareholders.

CHAPTER EIGHTEEN

Call to Action

Anyone Can Be a Leader

My call to action is to business leaders. Why? Because business leaders and entrepreneurs can become change agents in the world.

Moreover, I believe everyone can be a leader. No matter what field you are in, or what shape or size your business is, if you are a leader in your family, among your friends, in school, or just traveling through life: take action.

In my mind, action is quiet, subtle, inward, and yet powerful, because it resonates to everything and everyone around us.

I hope that I have inspired you not only on a business level, but also on a spiritual level, giving you practical ways to elevate your intention, connect to your own values, and prosper. You can see now how people, companies, and organizations can become truly values-based, and how in the long run, it actually makes you more profitable in so many ways.

Once you connect to your own values, you have an important leadership role to play in helping to motivate and connect the people around you to their personal values and the collective values you adopt as a company or organization.

When we believe in something bigger than ourselves and conduct ourselves accordingly—in all aspects of our lives, meaning in our private lives, in our business activities, and our philanthropy—we reach our highest potential.

In this way, you can see that values-based leadership goes way beyond just business. It is based on being mindful to your own values that are at the heart of your own vision and actions. Your values make you the type of person you are, the type of leader you want to be; and everyone can be a leader, each one in their own unique way.

Leaders inspire with their vision. They bring elevated ideas and transform them into reality. We have the power to change. We have the power to inspire. We have the power to make a difference. We all want the same things, we all want to grow and be fulfilled, live our dreams and passions, and at the same time be happy, healthy, and at peace.

So I challenge you to think not only of your future success, but of succeeding with a moral compass in your heart, and a state of mind of win-win, where everyone becomes winners. Some may say this is not possible, but I am here today to tell you that it is possible. Anything is possible when you put your mind and heart to it, and do it in a positive way.

So let's individually and collectively make the difference we want to see. A powerful difference, a positive one, a good one, one that is for the good of all.

CLOSING SECTION

The Doing Good Model:
Values Defined

Financial Freedom: The freedom (and the desire) to choose, based on responsibility and understanding of the framework of abilities and economic possibilities at any given moment.

Purity: The clarity of thoughts, intentions, and actions.

Being: Harmonious existence with all of the components that create the whole.

Inner Peace: An internal, personal, continuous, and constant process that leads us to a quiet place, balanced and tranquil within us.

Fulfillment: Realizing the self's full potential (while being at peace with our choices).

Vitality: An internal, driving energy that enables a dynamic pace of life, vibrancy, and constant renewal.

Giving: To give from a sincere, empowering, and true place.

Volunteering: Action in the community, based on inner strength and love for others.

Language & Communication: A range of channels that facilitate the sending and receiving of information, with synchronization, authenticity, respect, and precision, which lead to an understanding of the messages as they are.

Sustainability: Protecting and enhancing existence through economic, social, and environmental balance—for us and for the generations to come.

Added Value For Humanity: The courage and ability to lead to a better world by connecting between thought, emotion, and actions, and the fulfillment of the universal potential.

We Are All One: Each person has his or her uniqueness. All of us comprise the whole and constitute part of it.

Abundance: Recognizing that everything exists and responsible action for ensuring "what is."

The Doing Good Model:
At a Glance

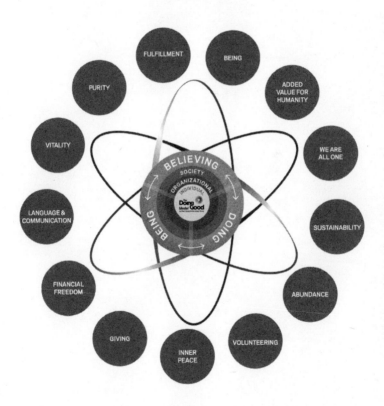

Acknowledgments

There are so many people whom I wish to thank that it would take another entire book for all the names. As I said in the dedication, you are all, each and every one of you, appreciated.

To my children, Jason, David, Cassie, and Daniel who give of themselves, both personally within our family as well as being part of our businesses and philanthropy.

To The Ted Arison Family Foundation Group, Management and Employees: With Jason's leadership, you are fulfilling my philanthropic dreams and creating true and lasting transformation.

To the Arison Investments Group and SAFO, Management and Employees: Especially Efrat Peled, who has, over the years, steadfastly overcome the challenges, making sure that my dream of values-based business is achieved and sustainable.

To Meir Wietchner and his team: For their commitment to the *Doing Good Model* and the expansion of it.

To my agent, Bill Gladstone, that through his dedication he has brought my work to audiences worldwide; to my publisher, BenBella, for believing in me and for their professionalism; to my editor, Simone Graham, who has worked wholeheartedly to simplify my vision; and to Finn Partners, especially Deborah Kohan, Amy Terpeluk, and their teams, for putting their heart together with their incredible work.

To all those who were interviewed, who gave of their stories and shared facts, whether named in the book or not, you know who you are. A special thanks to Ido Stern and Tamar Ben Ruby, and their teams for caring and doing everything possible for my books to be a success and for the messages in them to resonate out, creating the positive world we all want to see.

About the Author

Shari Arison is an American-Israeli businesswoman and philanthropist, owner of the global enterprise Arison Group, which operates in more than 40 countries across five continents to realize the vision of Doing Good through business and philanthropy.

The Arison Group's business arm, Arison Investments, operates in the fields of finance (Bank Hapoalim), infrastructure, real estate and renewable energy (Shikun & Binui), salt (Salt of the Earth), and water (Miya). Its philanthropic arm, The Ted Arison Family Foundation, houses the organizations Essence of Life, Goodnet, All One, and Ruach Tova that operates Arison's global initiative Good Deeds Day. She also initiated Matan, the Israeli United Way.

Arison created a unique values-based model, to bring fundamental human values to the core consciousness of businesses, organizations, and communities. Acknowledging the *Doing Good Model*, she was named Honorary Doctor of Humane Letters by George Mason University.

In 2010, Shari Arison received the America-Israel Friendship League's Partner for Democracy Award in recognition of her contribution to advancing economic relations between the USA and Israel. In 2011, and again in 2012, she was ranked by Forbes magazine as one of the World's Most Powerful Women, positioning her as a force of good in business and philanthropy. She was also ranked second on Forbes's list of the World's Greenest Billionaires, in recognition of her contributions to the environment, both in Israel and throughout the world, which she puts into practice in her business dealings.

Shari Arison is the author of international bestseller *Activate Your Goodness*, and *Birth: When the Spiritual and the Material Come Together*. She is the mother of four, a grandmother, and resides in Israel.

For more information, visit www.shariarison.com.

Books by Shari Arison

Material for Thought
Material for Thought is a voyage of spiritual and emotional development through art, through matter, the senses, colors, and textures. Each of us has our own uniqueness. Shari discovered creation and creativity deep within herself. Through art, she connected with the uniqueness in herself, because, for her, creation is art and art is creation. Shari invites you to see, feel, and experience the journey through art.

Activate Your Goodness: Transforming the World Through Doing Good
Activate Your Goodness: Transforming the World Through Doing Good is a practical guide for fulfilling the vision of doing good. The book presents the power of a good deed and gives practical tools for creating change

among people, communities and companies. The idea at its base is that if we begin to think good, speak good, and do good, we can create a better world.

Birth: When the Spiritual and Material Come Together

Birth: When the Spiritual and Material Come Together reveals to the reader the path Shari Arison travelled, in both the business and spiritual realms, and the insights she has reached with regard to the connection between the two. In this book, she seeks to share with us her moving personal journey and chart the way in which she sees the future.